Multiple Regression with Discrete Dependent Variables

POCKET GUIDES TO
SOCIAL WORK RESEARCH METHODS

Series Editor
Tony Tripodi, DSW
Professor Emeritus, Ohio State University

Determining Sample Size
Balancing Power, Precision and Practicality
Patrick Dattalo

Preparing Research Articles
Bruce A. Thyer

Systematic Reviews and Meta-Analysis
Julia H. Littell, Jacqueline Corcoran, and Vijayan Pillai

Historical Research
Elizabeth Ann Danto

Confirmatory Factor Analysis
Donna Harrington

Randomized Controlled Trials
Design and Implementation for
Community-Based Psychosocial Interventions
Phyllis Solomon, Mary M. Cavanaugh, and Jeffrey Draine

Needs Assessment
David Royse, Michele Staton-Tindall, Karen Badger,
and J. Matthew Webster

Multiple Regression with Discrete Dependent Variables
John G. Orme and Terri Combs-Orme

Developing Cross-Cultural Measurement
Thanh V. Tran

Intervention Research
Developing Social Programs
Mark W. Fraser, Jack M. Richman, Maeda J. Galinsky,
and Steven H. Day

JOHN G. ORME
TERRI COMBS-ORME

Multiple Regression with Discrete Dependent Variables

OXFORD
UNIVERSITY PRESS

2009

OXFORD
UNIVERSITY PRESS

Oxford University Press, Inc., publishes works that further
Oxford University's objective of excellence
in research, scholarship, and education.

Oxford   New York
Auckland   Cape Town   Dar es Salaam   Hong Kong   Karachi
Kuala Lumpur   Madrid   Melbourne   Mexico City   Nairobi
New Delhi   Shanghai   Taipei   Toronto

With offices in
Argentina   Austria   Brazil   Chile   Czech Republic   France   Greece
Guatemala   Hungary   Italy   Japan   Poland   Portugal   Singapore
South Korea   Switzerland   Thailand   Turkey   Ukraine   Vietnam

Published by Oxford University Press, Inc.
198 Madison Avenue, New York, New York 10016

www.oup.com

Oxford is a registered trademark of Oxford University Press

Library of Congress Cataloging-in-Publication Data

Orme, John G.
Multiple regression with discrete dependent variables / John G. Orme & Terri
Combs-Orme.
p. cm.
Includes bibliographical references and index.
ISBN 978-0-19-532945-2
1. Social service—Statistical methods.   2. Regression analysis.
I. Combs-Orme, Terri.   II. Title.
HV29.O76 2009
519.5′36—dc22
2008030809

9 8 7 6 5 4 3 2 1

Printed in the United States of America
on acid-free paper

*This book is dedicated to all our teachers who first inspired us,
and to our students, who continue to inspire us.*

Preface

I t is certainly a truism that to do a good job, you have to choose the right tool, whether the job involves home repair or data analysis. In some ways, we have reached a point in social work research, however, where the toolbox contains so many different and specialized tools that it can be difficult to select the appropriate one. Each data analysis method has numerous assumptions, options, exceptions, and limitations, but at the same time the availability of easy-to-use software tempts us to simply try everything until we get results that please us.

Most social work researchers' toolboxes contain linear regression, usually referred to as *multiple regression* or *ordinary least squares multiple regression*, and we frequently employ it. Linear regression is a versatile and powerful statistical method that can be used to model the effects of one or more independent variables (IVs) on a dependent variable (DV) (Cohen, Cohen, West, & Aiken, 2003; Fox, 2008). It can be employed to analyze data collected using diverse research designs, including experimental, quasi-experimental, and nonexperimental designs. It can also accommodate any type of IV. However, linear regression assumes (among other things) a continuous DV.

Continuous variables are quantitative variables that can take on any value within the limits of the variable. For example, distance, time, or length can have an infinite number of possible divisions between any two values, at least theoretically. On the other hand, both Cohen et al. (2003) and Nunnally and Bernstein (1994) note that by this strict mathematical

definition no empirically defined quantities would be considered continuous. That is, no measured variable is truly continuous. Nunnally and
Bernstein asserted that a variable could be treated as continuous if it can
assume more than 11 ordered values. By this definition, many dependent variables of interest to social workers are at least quasi-continuous.
These include, for example, scores on standardized scales such as those
that measure parenting attitudes, depression, family functioning, and
children's behavioral problems.

On the other hand, many DVs that interest us are discrete, not continuous. In contrast to continuous variables, **discrete variables** have a
finite number of indivisible values; they cannot take on all possible values
within the limits of the variable. Discrete variables include variables that
are dichotomous, polytomous, ordinal, or counts. **Dichotomous variables** have two categories that indicate whether an event has or has not
occurred, or that some characteristic is or is not present (e.g., placement in foster care coded *yes* or *no*). **Polytomous variables** have three
or more unordered categories (e.g., type of foster care placement coded
kin care, non-kin family care, group home care, or *institutional care*). **Ordinal variables** have three or more ordered categories (e.g., severity of child
abuse injury rated *none, mild, moderate,* or *severe*). **Count variables** indicate the number of times a particular event occurs, usually within some
time period (e.g., number of hospital visits per year), population size
(e.g., number of registered sex offenders per 100,000 population), or
geographical area (e.g., county or state).

It is our impression that many social work researchers and those in
related areas are not sufficiently familiar with the tools available for analyzing such variables, with perhaps the exception of logistic regression for
dichotomous DVs. Nor are they sufficiently aware of the similarities and
differences among these different models, considerations involved in the
selection of the most appropriate models, or interpretation and presentation of results from these models. This lack of broad knowledge about
multiple regression is unfortunate, because many important DVs cannot
or should not be modeled using linear regression.

The purpose of this book is to add a few new versatile tools to
your toolbox: to extend the knowledge of alternative regression models among social work researchers and those in related areas so that they
will be in a better position to accurately model important DVs of interest to the profession. To that end, in this book we will demonstrate the

ease with which these different regression models may be estimated and interpreted.

Organization and Overview of Chapters

The book has five chapters: (1) Introduction to Regression Modeling; (2) Regression With a Dichotomous Dependent Variable; (3) Regression With a Polytomous Dependent Variable; (4) Regression With an Ordinal Dependent Variable; and (5) Regression With a Count Dependent Variable.

In Chapter 1, you will find a very brief review of the key concepts of linear regression. Then, we provide an introduction to the **Generalized Linear Model** (GZLM), which extends the linear regression model to DVs that are not continuous and provides a unifying framework for analyzing the entire class of regression models in this book, including linear regression. Finally, this chapter provides a discussion of assumptions common to all regression models in this book.

Chapter 2 provides a foundation for the other regression models presented in the remainder of this book. In fact, regression models for dichotomous outcomes are the foundation from which these more complex models are derived (Long & Freese, 2006). Therefore, in this chapter, we introduce many of the concepts and principles of estimating, testing, and interpreting regression models that can be adapted to regression models presented in the remaining chapters. Consequently, this chapter is longer and more detailed than subsequent chapters, and we strongly advise that you read it carefully before turning to the remaining chapters.

Chapters 3 through 5 are largely self-contained and can be read in any order. However, each of these chapters assumes that you have read the first two chapters. In fact, although you can sit down with a glass of wine and read the book from front to back, it is not written for that purpose, and we expect many readers to pick it up when they need guidance in conducting specific analyses. Therefore, some of the material is repeated across these three chapters, to allow you to easily use the book this way.

In Chapters 2 through 5, you will find discussions of appropriate situations for use of the particular regression methods presented, steps in estimating the regression model, substantive interpretation and presentation of the results of the analysis, and procedures for examining the assumptions underlying the model. Special emphasis is placed throughout on interpretation of the regression parameters, because this is more challenging for methods other than linear regression, and it is where we often find the published research lacking.

You will see that Chapters 2 through 3 follow a similar format. We start by introducing a simple example with a single dichotomous IV using a cross-tabulation table (except in Chapter 5, where a comparison of means is more appropriate). Then, we use the familiar context of the cross-tabulation table to introduce methods for quantifying the strength and direction of the relationships between the variables. We follow by introducing the regression model, and then analyzing the example with the regression model and relating those results back to the cross-tabulation results. We hope that this link between the familiar and the new will be helpful for understanding the regression models.

In subsequent sections, we expand each regression model to include quantitative IVs (sometimes called **covariates**), polytomous IVs (sometimes called **factors**), multiple IVs, and curvilinear and interaction effects. (However, for the most part, we have kept the models we illustrate relatively simple for pedagogical purposes.) In the following section, we present the assumptions underlying each regression model and discuss the methods for examining the assumptions. Given the brevity of the book, there are a number of variations of the regression models that we cannot cover, but at the end of each chapter, we note especially important variations of the models and direct readers to accessible readings and Web sites on the subject. The end of each chapter provides instructions for using SPSS to estimate the regression model and a brief description of the MS Excel Workbooks we used to create figures and tables.

You will need to use simple calculations to create your own tables and graphs from the SPSS output to fully understand and present results in the most meaningful and parsimonious way. We use MS Excel to do this, and the MS Excel Workbooks we used to create the figures and tables in this book are available to you on the companion Web site of this book (www.oup.com/us/pocketguides). These workbooks also contain additional figures and tables not presented in this book, and we encourage you to peruse these workbooks.

We provide recent examples from social work research throughout the book (see Orme & Buehler [2001] for earlier examples). We also provide data from our own research on foster families and disadvantaged mothers to illustrate the regression models, and these data and the SPSS output for the analyses we present are available to you on the companion Web site of this book (www.oup.com/us/pocketguides). We illustrate these different models using SPSS because SPSS is relatively easy to use and widely known to social workers and those in related areas. Throughout the book, we also direct you to accessible, more detailed discussions and applications of the topics discussed.

Audience and Background of Readers

This book is not for students in beginning statistics classes, but you also do not need to be a statistician to use it productively. Good use of the material requires a working knowledge of sampling, design, and measurement. We assume that you have an applied knowledge of statistics, including understanding of estimation and hypothesis-testing and chi-squared tests, t-tests, analysis of variance and applied linear regression. Finally, we assume that you have a basic understanding of SPSS, including how to recode and compute new variables, how to construct scatter plots and histograms, and how to compute basic descriptive statistics.

We hope that this book will be useful as a textbook, perhaps as one text in a course on multiple regression (which is how we use this book). We also hope that this book will be useful to graduate students in the social sciences who have modest backgrounds in applied statistics and who would like an introduction to the GZLM and, more specifically, the most widely used multiple regression models for discrete dependent variables. Finally, we think that this book will be useful to researchers who did not encounter this material in graduate school but find themselves needing an applied understanding of how to use and interpret one or more of these regression models.

Glossaries of Statistical Terms

We define the major terms as we use them, but you might not be familiar with some of the terms that we do not define, or you might be interested in alternative definitions. The following provide glossaries of statistical terms that you might find useful:

http://www.statsoft.com/textbook/glosfra.html
http://www.geodata.soton.ac.uk/biology/lexstats.html
http://www.animatedsoftware.com/elearning/Statistics%20Explained/
    glossary/se_glossary.html
http://dorakmt.tripod.com/mtd/glosstat.html
http://davidmlane.com/hyperstat/glossary.html
http://www.stats.gla.ac.uk/steps/glossary/alphabet.html
http://www.ablongman.com/html/abrami/glossary/glossary.html

Statistical Symbols and Abbreviations

We use some abbreviations, and again we define them when we present them. The following is a summary of these that you can refer to as needed. Note that Greek letters symbolize **parameters** (a numerical characteristic of a population), and letters from the Latin alphabet symbolize **statistics** (a numerical characteristic of a sample).

a	Intercept
α	Intercept (alpha)
B	Unstandardized slope
β	Population slope and standardized sample slope (beta)
CI	Confidence interval
df	Degrees of freedom
DV	Dependent variable, Y
E	Exposure
e	Error (residual)
ε	Error (epsilon)
η	linear predictor (eta)
G	Link function
GLM	General linear model
GZLM	Generalized linear model
IIA	Independence of irrelevant alternatives
IRR	Incidence rate ratio
IV	Independent variable, X
k	Number of independent variables
λ	Rate (lambda)
L	Likelihood

L	Logit
Ln	Natural logarithm, to the base e
m	Number of categories in a DV
M	Mean
μ	Mean (mu)
Mdn	Median
ML	Maximum likelihood
N	Total number in a sample
n	Number in a subsample
OR	Odds ratio
OLS	Ordinary least squares
π	Probability (pi)
p	Probability
p̂	Estimated probability
ψ	Odds ratio (psi)
SD	Standard deviation
t	Threshold
τ	Threshold (tau)
VIF	Variance inflation factor
Z	Standardized variable

SPSS Instructions

We use SPSS 16.0 for the analyses reported in this book (http://spss.com/). Throughout each chapter, we present and discuss the SPSS output, and at the end of each chapter, we describe the steps used to obtain this output. You might want to consult SPSS *Advanced Models 16.0* (2007), which describes features of the SPSS Generalized Linear Model (GZLM) that was used in most of the analyses we report. Norusis (2006, 2007) is also a valuable source about estimating many of the regression models discussed in this book.

Companion Web site

The companion Web site for this book (www.oup.com/us/pocketguides) contains the following materials organized by chapter:

- SPSS (16.0) data set used in the chapter
- SPSS (16.0) output discussed in the chapter and related output not presented

- MS Excel Workbooks used to create figures (and in a few cases tables) presented in the chapter and related figures not presented

We hope that you will download these materials and use them with this book.

Acknowledgments

We thank Casey Family Programs (www.casey.org) for their support and for the valuable work they do with foster families.

We gratefully acknowledge our colleagues who were involved in the research illustrated in this book, including Cheryl Buehler, Daphne Cain, Donna Cherry, Tanya Coakley, Mary Ellen Cox, Gary Cuddeback, Michael McSurdy, Katie Rhodes, Alex Washington, and Elizabeth Wilson, with special thanks to Elizabeth Wilson for use of her dissertation data.

Special thanks to the PhD students who served as teaching assistants in JGO's statistics classes over the years: Juan Barthelemy, Donna Cherry, Tanya Coakley, Courtney Cronley, Gary Cuddeback, Mark Oliver, Andrea McCarter, and Wendy Wyse.

Finally, we acknowledge the foster parents and mothers who gave of their time and expertise to make our research possible.

Contents

Multiple Regression with Discrete Dependent Variables

1

Introduction to Regression Modeling

A researcher is interested in the effects of mothers' behavior during pregnancy on their newborns' birthweights. She considers maternal smoking and alcohol use, age and other demographics, and measures of psychological health, and she records infant birthweight in grams from birth certificates. Birthweight ranges from 750 g for a premature infant to over 4000 g, and because this outcome variable is continuous, she considers using multiple regression to analyze the data.

Multiple regression is used so frequently because it is so useful. It provides a way to understand the relationship of a set of independent variables (IVs) to a dependent variable (DV), and it allows us to explain or to predict a dependent variable.

Linear Regression

Although we assume that readers have a fundamental knowledge of linear regression, this section is designed as a brief review of some major concepts of linear regression presented in the context of an example. Even if you are well versed in linear regression, you may find a review of this section useful.

Throughout this book, you will see that when showing calculations we carry numbers out to three or four decimal places, although when we show results we will use two decimal places. We do this so that you can reproduce the calculations and get the same final results we obtain.

Bivariate Regression with a Dichotomous Independent Variable

Let us briefly discuss and illustrate linear regression by first examining the relationship between a single dichotomous IV and a continuous DV. We hypothesized that foster mothers who provide kinship care (we call them "kinship mothers," and the variable name is *KinCare*) would have greater potential to foster challenging children (e.g., children with emotional or behavioral problems) than non-kinship foster mothers, because kinship mothers would be motivated by the family relationship. We measured foster mothers' potential to foster challenging children with the Challenging Children Scale (variable name *CCS*). This scale has a potential range from 0 through 100, with higher scores indicating greater potential to foster challenging children (Orme, Cuddeback, Buehler, Cox, & Le Prohn, 2007). *CCS* has a fairly normal distribution, with $M = 58.69$ ($SD = 12.91$). *KinCare* is a dichotomous variable ($0 = no$, $1 = yes$). The sample contains 65 (21.38%) kinship care and 239 (78.62%) non-kinship care mothers.

Table 1.1 shows descriptive statistics, and Table 1.2 shows partial results of the linear regression. The *intercept* (or *Constant*, as shown in Table 1.2 directly from the SPSS output) is the mean value of the DV when the IV (or IVs in multiple regression) equals 0; in our example, this is the mean of *CCS* scores for non-kinship applicant mothers. The unstandardized slope (*Coefficient*, in SPSS output and the table) indicates the direction and amount of change in the DV associated with a one-unit increase in the IV, when controlling for other IVs; in our example,

Table 1.1 Descriptive Statistics for Challenging Children Scale as a Function of Kinship Care Status

Kinship Care	Mean	N	Std. Deviation	Variance
(0) No	57.877	239	12.911	166.698
(1) Yes	61.657	65	12.573	158.085
Total	58.686	304	12.913	166.738

Table 1.2 Coefficients

| Model | Unstandardized Coefficients | | Standardized Coefficients | | |
	B	Std. Error	Beta	t	Sig.
1 (Constant)	57.877	.831		69.684	.000
Kinship Care	3.779	1.796	.120	2.104	.036

a positive slope would indicate that the *CCS* mean is higher for kinship mothers, a negative slope would indicate the reverse, and the numerical value of the slope indicates the difference between the mean *CCS* scores for the two groups of mothers.

As shown in Table 1.2, *KinCare* and *CCS* scores are significantly related. The overall mean *CCS* score for kinship mothers equals 57.877, the intercept. Kinship mothers have higher scores on the *CCS* (3.78 points higher, to be exact), and so the mean of the *CCS* scores for these mothers equals 61.66 (57.877 + 3.779). However, R^2 (not shown) equals .014 ($F(1, 302) = 4.41, p = .036$), indicating that *KinCare* accounts for only 1.4% of the variance in *CCS*.

Inserting the intercept (57.877) and unstandardized slope (3.779) from Table 1.2 gives us the following regression equation:

$$\hat{Y} = 57.877 + (3.779)(X)$$

In this equation $\hat{Y}$ (*Y* "hat") represents the estimated mean value of the DV, and *X* represents the IV.

The estimated mean *CCS* score for non-kinship mothers (i.e., when $X = 0$) is:

$$57.877 = 57.877 + (3.779)(0)$$

The estimated mean *CCS* score for kinship mothers (i.e., when $X = 1$) is:

$$61.656 = 57.877 + (3.779)(1)$$

Compare these values to those in Table 1.1.

In linear regression, a *residual* is the difference between the observed (*Y*) and the estimated ($\hat{Y}$) values of the DV for a case ($Y - \hat{Y}$). The sample includes 304 foster mothers, and each case has a residual. For example, a non-kinship mother with a *CCS* score of 60 would have a residual of 2.12 (60.00 − 57.877), indicating an observed *CCS* score higher than expected.

Linear regression assumes (among other things) that the errors are normally distributed; this is equivalent to saying that the DV is normally distributed for all values of the IVs (Fox, 2008). Linear regression also assumes that the variance of the errors is the same for all values of the IVs.

Error is simply the total of all causes of a DV except the IVs included in the regression model—that is the excluded IVs, measurement error in the DV, and the random component of the DV (Fox, 2008). Residuals are sample estimates of the unknown population error, and linear regression assumes that residuals are normally distributed and that the variance of the residuals is the same for all values of the IVs. Of course, in this case we have only two values of the IV: 0 and 1. Let's take a look at these assumptions for this example.

Figure 1.1 shows a histogram of the distribution of residuals. As you can see, this distribution is approximately normal. Descriptive statistics

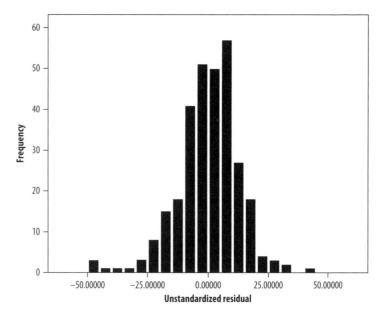

Figure 1.1 Histogram of Unstandardized Residuals

Table 1.3 Descriptive Statistics for Unstandardized Residuals by Kinship Care

Kinship Care	Mean	N	Std. Deviation	Variance
(0) No	0.000	239	12.911	166.698
(1) Yes	0.000	65	12.573	158.085
Total	0.000	304	12.819	164.329

for the residuals in Table 1.3 demonstrate approximately equal variances for the unstandardized residuals for kinship and non-kinship mothers.

Multiple Regression with Dichotomous and Continuous Independent Variables

Here we build on our example to illustrate multiple regression with both a dichotomous and a continuous IV. Earlier we saw that kinship mothers had greater potential to foster challenging children, but it is possible that the relationship between *KinCare* and *CCS* scores is due to something else entirely, for example the time mothers have available to foster (i.e., available time to foster is a **common cause** of both, and so the relationship is *spurious*). Specifically, we suspected that foster mothers who report that they have more time to foster would have greater potential to foster challenging children and also to provide kinship care, perhaps because they are more committed to *making* more time available. So, the research question examined here is this: Do kinship caregivers have greater potential to foster challenging children, controlling for available time to foster? To examine this question, we included a measure of available time to foster in our regression model, the Available Time Scale (variable name *ATS*). The *ATS* has a potential range of values from 0 through 100, with higher scores indicating more time to foster ($M = 77.28, SD = 12.73$).

Table 1.4 shows intercorrelations among the three variables. As hypothesized, ATS scores are correlated in the expected direction with both potential to foster challenging children (*CCS*) scores and *KinCare*.

KinCare was entered into the regression model in the first block, and *ATS* scores in the second. (When you enter variables one at a time, or in blocks, in a predetermined order dictated by the purpose and logic of the research questions, this is called *sequential* or *hierarchical* entry of variables [Cohen et al., 2003]) Tables 1.5, 1.6, and 1.7 show partial

Table 1.4 Correlations

		Challenging Children Scale	Kinship Care	Available Time Scale
Pearson Correlation	Challenging Children Scale	1.000	.120	.341
	Kinship Care	.120	1.000	.260
	Available Time Scale	.341	.260	1.000
Sig. (1-tailed)	Challenging Children Scale	—	.018	.000
	Kinship Care	.018	—	.000
	Available Time Scale	.000	.000	—
N	Challenging Children Scale	304	304	304
	Kinship Care	304	304	304
	Available Time Scale	304	304	304

Table 1.5 Model Summary

Model	R	R Square	Adjusted R Square	Std. Error of the Estimate	R Squared Change	F Change	df1	df2	Sig. F Change
1	.120	.014	.011	12.84028	.014	4.427	1	302	.036
2	.343	.118	.112	12.17008	.103	35.178	1	301	.000

Table 1.6 ANOVA

Model	Sum of Squares	df	Mean Square	F	Sig.
1 Regression	729.946	1	729.946	4.427	.036
Residual	49791.611	302	164.873		
Total	50521.556	303			
2 Regression	5940.220	2	2970.110	20.053	.000
Residual	44581.336	301	148.111		
Total	50521.556	303			

Table 1.7 Coefficients

Model	Unstandardized Coefficients		Standardized Coefficients		
	B	Std. Error	Beta	t	Sig.
1 (Constant)	57.877	.831		69.684	.000
Kinship Care	3.779	1.796	.120	2.104	.036
2 (Constant)	32.389	4.369		7.413	.000
Kinship Care	1.060	1.763	.034	.601	.548
Available Time Scale	.337	.057	.333	5.931	.000

results of the regression analysis. No statistically significant relationship exists between *KinCare* and *CCS* scores when controlling for *ATS* scores $(t(1, 301) = .60, p = .548$, Table 1.7). On the other hand, you see that the relationship between *ATS* and *CCS* scores *is* statistically significant when controlling for *KinCare* $(t(1, 301) = 5.93, p < .001)$. For every one-unit increase in *ATS* scores, *CCS* scores increase by .34, when controlling for *KinCare*, as indicated by the unstandardized *ATS* slope. For every one standard-deviation increase in *ATS* scores, *CCS* scores increase by .33 standard-deviation units, as indicated by the standardized *ATS* slope. R^2_{change} equals .103 (Table 1.5), indicating that the inclusion of *ATS* scores accounts for an additional 10.3% of variance in *CCS* scores. R^2 for the total model equals .118, indicating that 11.8% of the variance in *CCS* scores is accounted for by *KinCare* and *ATS* scores.

Inserting the intercept (32.389) and unstandardized slopes for *Kin-Care* (1.060) and *ATS* (.337) from Table 1.7 gives us the following regression equation:

$$\hat{Y} = 32.389 + (1.060)(X_{KinCare}) + (.337)(X_{ATS})$$

You could use this regression equation to estimate a *CCS* score for each case. Then, for each case, you would subtract the estimated *CCS* score from the observed *CCS* score to get the residual $(Y - \hat{Y})$. SPSS will do these calculations for you. Figure 1.2 shows a histogram of the distribution of residuals. This distribution is approximately normal.

Figure 1.3 shows a scatterplot with the residuals on the vertical axis and *ATS* scores on the horizontal axis. The variance of the unstandardized residuals is relatively constant across *ATS* scores.

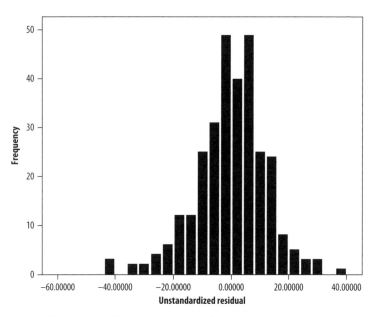

Figure 1.2 Histogram of Unstandardized Residuals

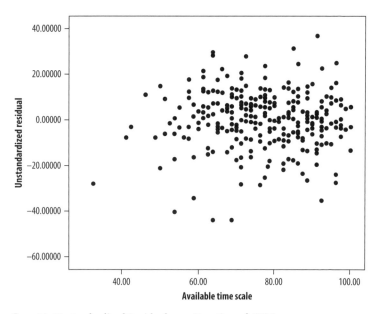

Figure 1.3 Unstandardized Residuals as a Function of *ATS* Scores

Model and Notation

Formally, the linear regression equation for a DV, Y, and a linear combination of IVs, X_1 through X_k, can be written as:

$$Y = \alpha + \beta_1 X_1 + \beta_2 X_2 + \ldots \beta_k X_k + \varepsilon$$

In this equation α (Greek letter *alpha*) (some authors use β_0) represents the population value of the *intercept*, which is the mean value of the DV when all IVs equal 0. Each IV is symbolized by X, and X_1 through X_k refer to specific values of IVs that vary from case to case. β_1 through β_k (Greek letter *Beta*) represent population values of the *slopes*, which indicate the direction and amount of change in the mean value of the DV associated with a one-unit increase in the associated IV, when controlling for the other IVs. Finally, ε (Greek letter *epsilon*) represents unexplained variation in the DV, typically called the *error term*.

The population values of the intercept and slope (the parameters) are unknown and estimated from sample data. The estimated regression model can be written as:

$$\hat{Y} = a + B_1 X_1 + B_2 X_2 + \ldots B_k X_k$$

$\hat{Y}$ (Y "hat") represents the estimated mean value of the DV; sometimes this is called the *conditional mean* because it depends on values of the IVs for each case. The estimated intercept is symbolized by a (some authors use B_0). Each IV is symbolized by X, and X_1 through X_k refer to specific values of IVs that vary from case to case. Each estimated slope is symbolized by B. Each IV has a slope, B_1 through B_k, and each slope indicates the direction and amount of change in the mean value of the DV associated with a one-unit increase in the IV, controlling for the other IVs.

When values of the DV are estimated for specific cases, frequently the estimated regression model is written as:

$$\hat{Y}_i = a + B_1 X_{1i} + B_2 X_{2i} + \ldots B_k X_{ki}$$

You will note that the only difference between this equation and the one above is the subscript i. The subscript i indicates that the equation is estimating values for specific cases ($i = 1$ for the first case, 2 for the second case, etc.). So, for example, $\hat{Y}_1$ represents the estimated value of the DV for the first case.

Additional Readings and Web Links

We have read a number of excellent books on linear regression. Keith (2006) is an especially good place to start. Cohen et al. (2003), Pedhazur (1997), and Fox (2008) are all readable, comprehensive texts.

You might find the following Web sites useful resources for linear regression:

http://www2.chass.ncsu.edu/garson/PA765/regress.htm
http://www.ats.ucla.edu/stat/SPSS/webbooks/reg/
http://mlrv.ua.edu/

The following Web sites also provide useful interactive exercises illustrating principles of linear regression:

http://www.ruf.rice.edu/~lane/stat_sim/reg_by_eye/index.html
http://www.civil.uwaterloo.ca/brodland/statistics/linear_regression.html
http://www.math.csusb.edu/faculty/stanton/m262/regress/regress.html
http://wise.cgu.edu/applets/Correl/correl.html
http://www.ruf.rice.edu/~lane/stat_sim/restricted_range/index.html

Generalized Linear Models (GZLM)

Linear regression is a member of a family of statistical models known as the *general linear model (GLM)*. The general linear model incorporates a number of different statistical models for use with one or more continuous DVs. The general linear model includes the *t*-test, ANOVA, and ANCOVA, and these single DV models are subsumed under linear regression. Common to these models are the assumptions of the following: a continuous DV; normally distributed independent errors with a constant variance; and a linear relationship between a linear combination of one or more IVs and one DV.

The *generalized linear model (GZLM)*, the topic we turn to next, extends the GLM to include discrete DVs (McCullagh & Nelder, 1989). Linear and other regression models described in this book, and a number of regression models not described in this book, are members of this family of regression models (Fox, 2008; Greene, 2008; McCulloch, Searle, & Neuhaus, 2008).

In the statistics literature *GLM* is used as the abbreviation for both the generalized linear model and the general linear model. Some authors also use *GLIM* as the abbreviation for the generalized linear model. We use *GZLM* as the abbreviation for the generalized linear model throughout this book to clearly distinguish it from the general linear model and to be consistent with SPSS, which uses *GZLM* as the abbreviation for the generalized linear model.

Linear regression is most appropriate with a continuous DV and normally distributed independent errors with a constant variance, and it is subsumed under the GZLM. The GZLM extends the linear regression model to DVs that are not continuous and to DVs that do not have normally distributed errors with a constant variance. (This is the "generalized" part of the GZLM.) The GZLM provides a framework for analyzing an entire class of models using unified techniques. At the same time, it uses many familiar ideas from linear regression.

The linear regression equation can be written as:

$$\mu = \alpha + \beta_1 X_1 + \beta_2 X_2 + \ldots \beta_k X_k$$

In this equation, μ (Greek letter *mu*) represents the population value of the mean of the DV.

In the language of the GZLM, the linear combination of the IVs, the right-hand side of this equation, is symbolized by η (Greek letter *eta*), and is called the *linear predictor*. The symbol η is just an abbreviation for the right-hand side of this equation. So, another way to express the linear regression model is:

$$\mu = \eta$$

Like all family members, GZLMs have a lot in common. Those familiar with linear regression will find many important similarities between linear regression and the regression models discussed in this book. In all of these regression models, (a) IVs are combined in a linear fashion (e.g., $\alpha + \beta_1 X_1 + \beta_2 X_2 + \ldots \beta_k X_k$); (b) a slope is estimated for each IV; (c) each slope has an accompanying test of statistical significance and a confidence interval; (d) each slope indicates the IV's independent contribution to the explanation or prediction of the DV; (e) the sign of each slope indicates the direction of the relationship; (f) IVs can be any level of measurement; (g) the same methods are used for coding categorical IVs (e.g., dummy coding, effect coding); (h) IVs can be entered simultaneously, sequentially, or using other methods (e.g., backward selection); (i) product terms can be used to test interactions; (j) powered terms (e.g., the square or cube of an IV) can be used to test curvilinearity; (k) overall model fit can be tested, as can incremental improvement in a model brought about by the addition or deletion of IVs (nested models); (l) residuals, leverage values, Cook's D, and other indices are used to diagnose model problems; and (m) multicollinearity can present problems in estimation and interpretation.

Population Distributions

We will call your attention to several basic differences between linear regression and the other regression models discussed in this book. One fundamental difference concerns the level of measurement of the DV. Linear regression is most appropriate with a continuous DV and normally distributed independent errors with a constant variance. Other regression models accommodate other types of DVs and errors with different distributions. Table 1.8 shows the assumed distributions and DVs for the regression models discussed in this book. All of these distributions are in what is known as the *exponential family of distributions* (which includes the normal, binomial, Poisson, multinomial, gamma, and other distributions).

Link Functions

Linear regression models the mean DV (μ) directly. The other regression models discussed in this book model a function of the mean DV through a "link function." The link function provides a unifying framework for

Table 1.8 Dependent Variables and Regression Models

DV	Regression	Link Name	Link Function	Inverse Link	Distribution
Continuous	Model Linear	Identity	μ	η	Normal
Unordered categorical (binary)	Binary logistic	Logit	$\ln(\mu/(1-\mu))$	$\mu = e^{\eta}/(1+e^{\eta})$	Binomial
Unordered categorical (polytomous)	Multinomial logistic	Logit	$\ln(\mu/(1-\mu))$	$\mu = e^{\eta}/(1+e^{\eta})$	Multinomial
Ordered categorical	Ordinal logistic	Logit	$\ln(\mu/(1-\mu))$	$\mu = e^{\eta}/(1+e^{\eta})$	Multinomial
Count	Poisson	Log	$\ln(\mu)$	$\mu = e^{\eta}$	Poisson
Count	Negative binomial	Log	$\ln(\mu)$	$\mu = e^{\eta}$	Negative Binomial

Note. This does not include the full range of GZLMs.

analyzing the entire class of regression models in this book, including linear regression. The link function is what makes it possible to model DVs that are not continuous, do not have normally distributed errors, do not have constant variance, and do not have a linear relationship with a linear combination of the IVs.

Usually the link function is designated $g(\mu)$, where g represents some function. For example, Poisson regression is used to model DVs that are counts (e.g., number of children adopted), as discussed in Chapter 5. Poisson regression models the natural log of the mean count, $ln(\mu)$, not the mean count itself. The function, in this example the log, links the DV to the linear combination of the IVs, η (i.e., $\alpha + \beta_1 X_1 + \beta_2 X_2 + \ldots \beta_k X_k$). This particular link function is called the *log link*. (If you are not familiar with logarithms, we urge you to read the discussion of logarithms in Appendix B.)

Different regression models have different link functions, and the appropriate link function and regression model depend on the assumed distribution of the errors. Table 1.8 shows the link functions for regression models discussed in this book. You will note in Table 1.8 that in linear regression $g(\mu)$ equals μ; no link is required, and this is known as the *identity function*.

The relationships between $g(\mu)$ and η are assumed to be linear in the regression models discussed in this book. The link function makes it possible to model DVs that have nonlinear relationships with the linear combination of the IVs. The link function transforms the relationship between the mean DV (μ) and the linear combination of the IVs (η) so the relationship is linear, just as it is in linear regression. (This is the "linear" part of the generalized linear model.)

In Poisson regression, for example, a linear relationship between the log of the estimated mean count and the linear combination of the IVs is assumed. This can be written as:

$$\ln(\mu) = \alpha + \beta_1 X_1 + \beta_2 X_2 + \ldots \beta_k X_k$$

Or, for short, it can be written as:

$$\ln(\mu) = \eta$$

This is read as "the natural log of the mean equals the linear predictor."

Let's take an example. Suppose you are interested in the relationship between a linear combination of IVs and the number of children adopted, a count variable. Figure 1.4 illustrates the hypothetical

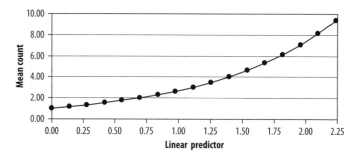

Figure 1.4 Mean Count as a Function of Linear Predictor

Table 1.9 Relationship Between the Linear Predictor, Mean, and Natural Log of the Mean

Linear Predictor	Mean Number of Children Adopted	Natural Logarithm of the Mean Number of Children Adopted
0.00	1.0000	0.0000
0.14	1.1500	0.1398
0.28	1.3225	0.2795
0.42	1.5209	0.4193
0.56	1.7490	0.5590
0.70	2.0114	0.6988
0.84	2.3131	0.8386
0.98	2.6600	0.9783
1.12	3.0590	1.1181
1.26	3.5179	1.2579
1.40	4.0456	1.3976
1.54	4.6524	1.5374
1.68	5.3503	1.6771
1.82	6.1528	1.8169
1.96	7.0757	1.9567
2.10	8.1371	2.0964
2.24	9.3576	2.2362

relationship between a linear combination of IVs and the mean number of children adopted. Table 1.9 shows the data used to create this figure. As you can see, this relationship is not linear. For example, the mean number of children adopted increases by .17 when the linear predictor goes from .14 to .28 (an increase of .14), but it increases by 1.06 when the linear predictor goes from 1.96 to 2.10 (an increase of .14).

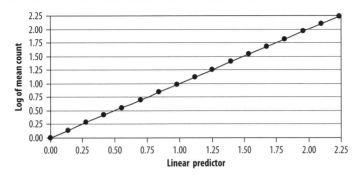

Figure 1.5 Log of Mean Count as a Function of Linear Predictor

Figure 1.5 illustrates the relationship between the linear predictor and the natural logarithm of the mean number of children adopted. As you can see, this relationship is linear.

Functions of the DV like $\ln(\mu)$ can transform a non-linear relationship to a linear relationship. However, values such as $\ln(\mu)$ are difficult to interpret because they do not have intuitive or substantive meaning. For example, the mean number of children adopted has intuitive and substantive meaning, but the log of the mean number of children adopted does not. Inverse functions, functions that undo the original function, can be applied to values such as $\ln(\mu)$ to obtain meaningful values of the DV, such as the mean number of children adopted.

Let's take an example of a familiar inverse function, and then we'll turn to one that might not be familiar to you. Take the square root of a number; for example, the square root of 4 is 2 ($\sqrt{4} = 2$). To get back to the original number, you just square the value of the square root ($2^2 = 4$). Squaring the number does the reverse of taking the square root, and in mathematics this is called an **inverse function**. Table 1.8 shows inverse functions for the regression models discussed in this book.

The *exponential function* is the inverse of the natural log, and it is written as e^x or $\exp(x)$. For x, just insert the value of η (i.e., $\alpha + \beta_1 X_1 + \beta_2 X_2 + \ldots \beta_k X_k$). This is written as: e^η or $\exp(\eta)$. This is read as "the base of the natural log raised to the power of the linear predictor."

So, again, the Poisson regression model can be written as:

$$\ln(\mu) = \eta$$

where η is the linear predictor and $\ln(\mu)$ is the log of the mean count, a value that does not have intuitive or substantive meaning. When you exponentiate η you get the mean count, μ (e.g., mean number of children adopted), a value that does have intuitive and substantive meaning:

$$\mu = e^{\eta}$$

The exponential function is central to all regression models discussed in this book, as you can see from Table 1.8. Exponentiating estimated values of the linear predictor, η, is key to interpreting and presenting results of all GZLMs. You need to know how to use the exponential function to obtain meaningful values of the DV, such as the mean number of children adopted, and you will need to do this for all of the GZLMs discussed in this book. Apply the exponential function to several values of the linear predictor from Table 1.9 to make sure that you know how to do this (e.g., $e^0 = 1.00$, $e^{.70} = 2.01$); that is, "exponentiate" values of the linear predictor. If you are using a calculator, enter the value (e.g., 0 or .70), press your "2nd" key, and press e^x (This procedure is somewhat different for some calculators). If you are using MS Excel, the mathematical function is $\exp(x)$.

Maximum Likelihood Estimation

The intercept and slopes obtained from a regression analysis are estimates of population values (i.e., parameters). Linear regression parameters are estimated in a way that minimizes the sum of the squared differences between the observed and estimated values of the DV. That is, the intercept and slopes are determined in such a way that the sum of the squared residuals is as small as possible. No other values of the slopes and intercept would result in a lower value for the sum of the squared residuals. This is called *ordinary least squares* (OLS) estimation, which is why linear regression oftentimes is called *OLS regression*.

A different method, *maximum likelihood* (ML), is used to estimate parameters for the regression models described in this book. ML estimates are values of the parameters that have the greatest likelihood (i.e., the maximum likelihood) of generating the observed sample data if the assumptions of the model are true (Long & Freese, 2006). For example, suppose you have no idea of the "real" probability of obtaining "heads" in the flip of a coin. You flip it 10 times and it comes up heads four times.

The estimated probability of heads that gives the maximum likelihood of producing the observed sample data is .40. Given the sample results, the likelihood is much less that the population probability is, for example, .10 or .90.

The probability of the observed sample data, given the parameter estimates, is known as the *likelihood*, typically abbreviated *L*. A good regression model is one that results in a high likelihood of the observed sample data (Norusis, 2007). The likelihood, *L*, is used in the generation of maximum likelihood estimates, and it is also used to test hypotheses about model parameters.

You may wonder how the outcomes differ for these two estimation methods. Since OLS methods cannot be used with the types of models we discuss in this book, we cannot answer that question. Both methods *can* be used with linear regression, however, and when the assumptions of linear regression are met, the outcomes are identical.

Test Statistics

The *t*-statistic is used to test hypotheses about individual slopes with linear regression, but the *Wald statistic* or *likelihood ratio* χ^2 typically is used with other regression models described in this book. Likewise, while the *F* statistic is used to test hypotheses about overall and nested models in linear regression, the likelihood ratio χ^2 is used for these purposes with the regression models discussed in this book. If you understand statistical tests in linear regression, it is a small step to apply similar techniques to other regression models discussed in this book.

Model Evaluation

Before you test hypotheses or interpret substantive results of any regression model, linear or otherwise, you should examine how well your regression model fits your data, that is, how effectively the model describes the DV. You will want to test the overall model, and often you will also want to compare different models. You also need to know if some individual cases are not well explained by the estimated model, or if some cases exert undue influence on the estimation of the model. Finally, you will want to know how well your model explains your DV overall.

One way to think about the quality of your regression model is to consider how closely the values of the DV estimated from your regression model ($\hat{Y}$) correspond to the observed values (Y) (Gill, 2001). The closer the correspondence, the better your model is at describing reality. In linear regression, R^2 is the squared correlation between estimated and observed values of the DV, and so it provides a direct measure of the quality of your regression model. For the regression models described in this book, there is no exact counterpart with the same properties as R^2. A number of analogs to R^2 exist, but none is in standard use and each may give different results (DeMaris, 2004).

In linear regression, we typically examine various types of residuals (e.g., unstandardized, standardized, and studentized) and leverage values to identify individual cases that are not explained well by the estimated model. Statistics such as Cook's D are examined to identify cases that exert undue influence on the estimation of the regression model. Comparable statistics are available for the regression models discussed in this book. We will discuss and illustrate these statistics and issues in subsequent chapters.

Sample Size

Sample size is an important determinant of the statistical power of tests of hypotheses and the precision with which parameters are estimated. ML estimation is known to work well with large samples. However, we do not have clear and agreed-upon guidelines for deciding just what sample size is necessary for ML estimation. Long and Freese (2006) provided some tentative working guidelines, advising that it is risky to use ML estimation with samples of fewer than 100 no matter the number of estimated parameters, and that you also should have at least 10 cases per estimated parameter. So, for example, regression models with fewer than 10 IVs would require a sample of at least 100, and models with more than 10 IVs would require larger samples (e.g., a model with 12 IVs would require a sample size of at least 120). However, little variation in the DV or considerable multicollinearity results in the need for samples larger than the suggested minimums. Finally, some regression models may require samples larger than the suggested minimums; in particular, this is true for the ordinal regression models we discuss in Chapter 4.

Additional Readings and Web Links

A number of good books discuss the GZLM. Applied researchers will find Hoffmann (2004) an especially good place to start learning about the GZLM and more specific regression models encompassed by the GZLM. Cohen et al. (2003) also provide a good introduction to the GZLM, and applied researchers interested in the GZLM and the models encompassed by it should read DeMaris (2004), Fox (2008), and Long's work (Long, 1997; Long & Cheng, 2004; Long & Freese, 2006). Hardin and Hilbe (2007) and Long and Freese both provide extensive treatment of the GZLM in the context of the statistical program STATA.

You might also find the following Web sites useful for learning more about the GZLM and the more specific regression models encompassed by the GZLM:

http://www.statsoft.com/textbook/stglz.html
http://userwww.sfsu.edu/~efc/classes/biol710/Glz/Generalized
    %20Linear%20Models.htm
http://www.education.man.ac.uk/rgsweb/EDUC61022.html
http://socserv.mcmaster.ca/jfox/Courses/soc740/index.html
http://www.unc.edu/courses/2006spring/ecol/145/001/docs/lectures/
    lecture20.htm
http://www.ed.uiuc.edu/courses/EdPsy490AT/lectures/
    4glm1-ha-online.pdf
http://www.gseis.ucla.edu/courses/ed231c/notes.html

Also, GZLM data sets are available at:

http://www.sci.usq.edu.au/staff/dunn/Datasets/tech-glms.html

Common Assumptions

All regression models have assumptions, and violation of these assumptions can result in a number of undesirable consequences. For example, the effects of IVs might be over- or underestimated (i.e., *biased*). Parameter estimates might be *inefficient* (vary relatively more from sample to sample) or *inconsistent* (have sampling distributions whose variability does not decrease with larger samples) (Fox, 2008; Long, 1997). Consequently, the assumptions underlying a regression model should be examined carefully before the model is used and the results are interpreted.

Linear regression is most appropriate with a continuous DV, and it assumes that the population values of the errors are independent and normally distributed with a constant variance and a linear relationship between a linear combination of one or more IVs and one DV. Other regression models make other assumptions about characteristics of the DVs and the distributions of the errors. We will discuss assumptions unique to the particular types of regression covered in subsequent chapters. However, all regression models discussed in this book have a common set of assumptions (Gill, 2001).

Correct Model Specification

A regression equation is a mathematical representation—a model—of what and how IVs are related to your DV. You should ask yourself some general questions when you construct your regression model, and these questions are central to the correct estimation and interpretation of any regression model (Cohen et al., 2003; Pedhazur, 1997):

- Have you included the relevant IVs in your regression model?
- Have you excluded the irrelevant IVs?
- Do the IVs that you have included have linear or nonlinear relationships with your DV (or some function of your DV, as is assumed with the models discussed in this book)?
- Are one or more of your IVs moderated by other IVs (i.e., are there interaction effects)?

Including the Relevant Variables and Excluding the Irrelevant Ones

Your first decisions in testing a model involve variable specification, and it is at this step that you use theory and the research literature to direct your attention to the most meaningful IVs. These variables can then be included in the model to provide the largest possible meaningful model for initial consideration (Kleinbaum & Klein, 2002). It is important not to omit variables that are crucial to the phenomenon; a model that does not include the relevant variables may produce results that look reasonable but that are *misspecified*. That is, if important variables are omitted, the regression coefficients you obtain may not accurately estimate the relationships among the variables.

For example, suppose you leave out an IV that is a common cause of your DV and one or more of your IVs (Cohen et al., 2003; Keith, 2006). (Sometimes these variables are referred to as *confounders*) (Hosmer & Lemeshow, 2000). In our linear regression example, we hypothesized that available time to foster influenced both potential to foster challenging children and whether or not mothers provided kinship care. We found a relationship between kinship care and potential to foster challenging children when we did not control for available time to foster, but not when we controlled for this presumed common cause. If we had omitted available time to foster from our regression model, we would have been left with a false impression about the effect of kinship care on the potential to foster challenging children. That is, the relationship between kinship care and potential to foster challenging children was confounded by available time to foster, and so the relationship was spurious. (Note that earlier the unstandardized slope for kinship care went from 3.78 to 1.06 when controlling for available time to foster. That is, the slope for kinship care was biased when available time to foster was excluded.).

> Linear regression assumes that the IVs and the error are independent in the population. Correlations of one or more IVs with the residuals indicate a violation of this assumption. The violation of this assumption implies the omission of an IV that is associated with one or more of the IVs that are included (Hoffmann, 2004).

On the other hand, you should not include irrelevant variables because you risk reducing your statistical power and increasing the width of confidence intervals for your regression parameters. This is especially problematic with small samples and even more so in areas without well-developed theories.

Including Relevant Interaction Terms

An interaction occurs when the effect of one IV (*focal variable*) is conditional on the values of one or more other IVs (*moderator variable*). The focal variable is the IV whose effect on the DV is thought to vary as a function of the moderator variable. The effect of the focal variable is said to be *conditional* on the moderating variable(s) (Jaccard, 2001).

For example, suppose you hypothesize that the effect of available time to foster (the *focal* variable) is different for non-kinship and kinship foster mothers (kinship care is the *moderator* variable). More specifically, available time might be less important for kinship foster mothers because they plan to foster children from their own families, whether or not they have the time. You model interactions in much the same way in all regression models: compute a new variable, the cross-product of the focal and moderator variables, and enter the new computed variable sequentially into the regression model. However, interactions are a bit more work to present and interpret for the regression models discussed in this book, given the nonlinear relationships between the IVs and the DV (e.g., Jaccard, 2001). We will come back to this issue in subsequent chapters.

Including Relevant Curvilinear Terms

Linear regression and all regression models discussed in this book assume that the relationship between the linear combination of the IVs (η) and some function of the mean DV (μ) is linear. Poisson regression, for example, assumes that the relationship between the linear combination of the IVs and the log of the mean DV is linear (although the relationship between the linear combination of the IVs and the DV is not linear).

You model curvilinear relationships in much the same way in all regression models; compute polynomials for continuous predictors (e.g., squared or cubic terms), and enter the computed variables into the regression model. We will come back to this issue in subsequent chapters.

Final Thoughts on Model Specification

How do you achieve a balance between comprehensiveness and parsimony? Your substantive knowledge of the theory and previous research in the area must guide your selection of variables, and the steps you take in making those decisions should be articulated. For example, information is often not provided in research reports as to how variables were chosen for the initial model, how variables were selected for the final model, and how effect modifiers and confounders were assessed for their roles in the final model. Without meaningful information about the modeling strategy used, it is difficult to assess the validity of the results.

Moreover, you cannot divorce the issue of model specification from design issues. Issues related to model specification and interpretation are more difficult with non-experimental research, because we cannot be certain what other factors might be influencing the DV. Statistical control cannot resolve this problem completely, even when we are aware of the problematic variables.

Variables Measured without Error

Linear regression and all of the regression models discussed in this book assume that the variables included in the regression analysis are measured without error. This is a limitation of regression models, given that most often our variables contain some measurement error.

Independent Errors

Imagine that you doubled your sample size by entering data for each case twice. If you did this you would have pairs of cases that were exactly the same. Values of the DV would be the same for each pair of "matched" cases, and the error for each pair (i.e., the difference between observed and expected values of the DV) would be the same. Linear regression and all regression models discussed in this book assume that the errors for each case are independent from the errors of all others. That is, the errors for any subset of cases are not related with each other. The errors for the "matched" cases in the example just discussed would be exactly the same, so this assumption would be violated.

This assumption can be understood most easily by considering some common examples of violations. Suppose you examined the effect of parenting practices on behavioral problems of children and you collected reports of parenting practices and behavioral problems from both parents in two-parent families. Couples usually interact with each other around these issues, and they share a common history and oftentimes similar perspectives and values regarding these issues. So, even though these pairs of "matched" cases would not be identical, the errors within couples probably are not completely independent.

As another example, suppose you collected information from only one parent per family, but you collected information about two or more children per family. Children from the same family usually have many things in common in terms of parenting practices and behavioral problems, and so errors for groups of two or more children within the same family also probably are not completely independent.

Finally, suppose you studied the effects of leader behaviors on group cohesion in small groups, and you collected information about leader behaviors and group cohesion from all members of each group. Members within each group share a common history of leader behaviors and group cohesion, and so errors within each group probably are not independent.

One thing shared by each of these examples is that individuals from whom the DVs were measured were not sampled independently. Couples were sampled as couples, not as individuals. Children were sampled from families, not independently as individuals. Group members were sampled because they belonged to a common group, not as individuals. That is, the method used to collect data leads to the lack of independence. So, although there are graphical and statistical ways to check whether errors are independent, for the most part this depends on how you collect your data, and you should be aware of this when you collect your data.

Finally, although linear regression and all regression models discussed in this book assume that the errors for each case are independent from the errors of all others, it is important to note that these models have been extended to allow for the analysis of repeated measurements or other correlated observations such as multilevel data (e.g., Gelman & Hill, 2007; McCulloch et al., 2008). However, these extensions are beyond the scope of this book.

No Perfect Multicollinearity

Linear regression and all of the regression models discussed in this book assume the absence of perfect multicollinearity. *Multicollinearity* refers to the situation where strong linear relationships exist among IVs. It does not have anything whatsoever to do with your DV. Multicollinearity occurs when highly related IVs are included in a regression model as, for example, might occur when different measures of the same construct are included as IVs in a regression model or when highly intercorrelated demographic characteristics are included.

You can think of multicollinearity as the amount of variance accounted for in each IV by the remaining IVs. With only two IVs, this is just the squared correlation between them (sometimes just called *collinearity*).

Perfect multicollinearity exists when an IV is predicted perfectly by a linear combination of the remaining IVs. When perfect multicollinearity exists, the slope for that IV cannot be computed properly. Another way to think about this is that neither of these IVs adds anything to the explanation of the DV after the other is entered.

High levels of multicollinearity (e.g., R^2 of .80 or more for one or more IVs) may pose problems, and very high levels of multicollinearity (e.g., R^2 of .90 or more for one or more IVs) may pose serious problems (Cohen et al., 2003; Fox, 2008). Slopes may not be statistically significant, even if they are quite large. Alternatively, the slopes may indicate a negative instead of a positive relationship (or *vice versa*). Standard errors may be inflated and the width of confidence intervals increased. The overall regression model may be statistically significant while none of the individual IVs is significant. However, problematic levels of multicollinearity may be a relatively rare problem in social science applications of linear models; small samples, insufficient variability in IVs, and weak relationships between IVs and DVs are more likely sources of imprecision in our estimates of the effects of IVs on DVs (Fox, 2008).

One of two related measures of multicollinearity typically is computed, reported, and interpreted for each IV in a regression model to identify problematic levels of multicollinearity: *tolerance* or the *variance inflation factor (VIF)*. Tolerance is the amount of variance in an IV not accounted for by the remaining IVs $(1 - R^2)$. Tolerance values of .10 or less are considered problematic (low tolerance values are undesirable) (Cohen et al., 2003). VIF is 1/tolerance, and VIF values of 10 or more (equal to tolerance values of .10 or less) are considered problematic (DeMaris, 2004). Cohen et al. caution that less extreme tolerance values also may be problematic, however.

Multicollinearity is relatively easy to detect, but less easy to remedy in a satisfactory fashion (Fox, 2008). For example, IVs may be deleted or combined, especially in cases where they clearly measure the same construct, although this might lead to **model misspecification**. Additional data may be collected, but usually this is impractical. Alternative statistical methods may be employed, but for some of the regression models in this book there are no easy alternative statistical methods, some of the alternatives may cause more problems then they solve, and no single model can be recommended in all situations. Nevertheless, multicollinearity should always be checked before interpreting a multiple regression model in order to properly interpret model results.

Limitations of Regression Models

While regression models are useful, they do have inherent limitations. First, the accuracy of multiple regression depends on whether the model includes all the relevant variables (as discussed earlier). If this assumption is untrue, the results of the regressions are suspect. In reality, of course, it is difficult to know all of the relevant variables, but in-depth knowledge of the substantive area is an important start.

Second, statistical analyses are useful for understanding aggregate data, but they cannot explain individual differences. This is a rule from Statistics 101—but it always bears repeating.

Third, an analysis with only a small number of observations may be unduly influenced by the characteristics of one or two individual cases. Fortunately, you can determine if this has occurred, and we discuss many of the ways to do this in subsequent chapters.

Finally, although cause–effect relationships are often implicit in regression models, the validity of inferences about cause and effect is determined by factors external to the data analysis. In particular, the research design must be considered carefully in making such inferences. A comprehensive discussion of these issues is beyond the scope of this book but, for example, see Shadish, Cook, and Campbell (2002).

SPSS Instructions

Linear Regression

- Start SPSS 16 and open the Chapter 1 data set.
- From the menus choose:
  Analyze
  Regression
  Linear...
- Select a continuous DV (e.g., *CCS*) and click the arrow button to move it to *Dependent*.
- Select IVs (e.g., *KinCare, ATS*) and click the arrow button to move them to *Independent(s)*.
- Use *Next* to enter IVs sequentially, if desired.

- Click *Statistics* and then click *Estimates, Confidence intervals, Model fit, R squared change, Descriptives, Collinearity diagnostics,* and *Casewise diagnostics.* Click *Continue.*
- Click *Plots* and then click *Histogram.* Select a type of residual (e.g., *SRESID,* which are *studentized residuals*) and click the arrow button to move it to *Y,* and select *ZPRED* (*standardized predicted values*) and move it to *X.* Click *Continue.*
- Click *Save* and then click *Studentized, Cooks,* and *Leverage values.* Click *Continue.*
- Click *OK* to get the results.

Note: After you run the analysis, save the data set, which now contains new variables that you can use to create index plots (and for other purposes).

Excel Workbooks

This workbook shows how we created the data and graphs for Figures 1.4 and 1.5: eta, mu, ln(mu).xls

2

Regression with a Dichotomous Dependent Variable

A researcher has a simple question: Did it happen, or did it not? Has the spouse abuser reoffended or not? Has the foster child been reunited with her family or not? These outcomes are dichotomous. That is, dichotomous variables have two categories that indicate whether an event has or has not occurred, or that some characteristic is or is not present. To simplify, we will just refer to "events" in this chapter. These variables are also called *binary* or sometimes *binomial* (the assumed underlying distribution). Social workers and those in related disciplines frequently conduct research with dichotomous DVs.

For example, we have investigated whether foster home applicants are subsequently licensed to foster or not (Orme et al., 2006) and whether or not mothers have used corporal punishment to discipline their infants (Combs-Orme & Cain, 2008).

In this chapter, we discuss the use of **binary logistic regression** (also known simply as *logistic regression* or sometimes as *logit regression*), a versatile and popular method for modeling relationships between a dichotomous DV and multiple IVs. Binary logistic regression extends linear regression to the situation where the DV is dichotomous (Bagley, White, & Golomb, 2001; Cohen et al., 2003; DeMaris, 2004; Hoffmann, 2004; Hosmer & Lemeshow, 2000; Jaccard, 2001; Kleinbaum & Klein, 2002; Long, 1997; Long & Freese, 2006; Norusis, 2006; Pampel, 2000).

It can also be used to analyze results from numerous types of designs, including, for example, case-control studies, cohort studies, complex sample surveys, clinical trials, and repeated measurements or other correlated observations such as multilevel data (Gelman & Hill, 2007; Hosmer & Lemeshow, 2000; Kleinbaum & Klein, 2002; McCulloch et al., 2008; Piantadosi, 2005).

Binary logistic regression has a lot in common with other regression models presented in the remainder of this book. In fact, logistic regression models for dichotomous outcomes are the foundation from which these more complex models are derived (Long & Freese, 2006). Except for linear regression, binary logistic regression probably is used more than any other regression model. Therefore, in this chapter, we introduce many of the concepts and principles of estimating, testing, and interpreting regression models that can be adapted to regression models presented in the remaining chapters. Consequently, this chapter is longer and more detailed than the subsequent chapters, and we strongly advise you to read it carefully before turning to the remaining chapters. If you are not familiar with logarithms, we urge you to read the discussion of logarithms in Appendix B before reading this chapter.

Chapter Example

In this chapter, we discuss and illustrate binary logistic regression by examining variables that influence foster families' plans to continue fostering or not. The sample includes 131 foster families (Rhodes, Orme, Cox, & Buehler, 2003a).

Families' reports of whether they planned to continue fostering or not make up the DV, and we coded families who did not plan to continue fostering as 0 and those who did plan to continue as 1. (It is customary to code the category of greatest interest as 1 and the other category as 0 because this makes it easier to interpret binary logistic regression results.) This outcome concerns whether or not families say they plan to continue fostering, not whether they actually continue, but for simplicity we just refer to the DV as *continuation*. The variable name in the data set and output is *ContinueFostering*. A total of 60 (45.80%) families in our sample reported that they did not plan to continue fostering, and 71 (54.20%) did plan to continue.

We will analyze the effects of three IVs at one point or another: marital status, number of family resources, and county of residence. Marital status (variable name *Married*) is a dichotomous variable that refers to whether a foster family was headed by an unmarried single parent (coded 0) or by two parents who were married (coded 1). The sample contains 49 (37.40%) one-parent families and 82 (62.60%) two-parent families.

Number of resources (variable name *Resources*) is the cumulative number of different types of family resources, both social (such as education) and material (such as high income). It has a fairly normal distribution, with $M = 6.60$ ($SD = 1.93$), and a range from 2 through 11.

County of residence (variable name *County*) is a multicategorical variable with three categories: Davidson, Hamilton, and Knox. The sample contains 46 (35.11%) families from Davidson County, 22 (16.79%) families from Hamilton County, and 63 (48.09%) families from Knox County.

Cross-Tabulation and Chi-Squared Test

We start by examining a simple research question: *Are two-parent families more likely to continue fostering than one-parent families?* We might expect this to be so for a number of reasons, and it's an important question for foster care agencies. A cross-tabulation table and chi-squared test let us answer this question and provide a good starting point for understanding binary logistic regression.

 Before you estimate a binary logistic regression model, cross-tabulate your DV with each of your categorical IVs to check for empty cells. If there are empty cells, consider collapsing or eliminating categories if it is justified theoretically.

Cross-Tabulation

The relationship between marital status and continuation of fostering is statistically significant [$\chi^2(1, N = 131) = 5.65, p = .017$]. As shown in Table 2.1, a higher percentage of two-parent families (62.20%) than single-parent families (40.82%) planned to continue fostering.

Table 2.1 Plan to Continue Fostering as a Function of Marital Status

| | | | *Married* | | |
			(0) Not Married	*(1) Married*	*Total*
Continue Fostering	(0) Not Continue	Count	29	31	60
		% within Married	59.18	37.80	45.80
	(1) Continue	Count	20	51	71
		% within Married	40.82	62.20	54.20
Total		Count	49	82	131
		% within Married	100.00	100.00	100.00

In binary logistic regression, the effects of IVs on the DV are interpreted and presented in terms of probabilities, odds, and odds ratios, so we now turn to a discussion of these concepts.

Probabilities

Think of the percentages in Table 2.1 as proportions (e.g., 62.20% as .6220). Then, think of the proportions as probabilities, where $\hat{p}$ is the estimated probability that the event will occur (*continue*) and $1 - \hat{p}$ is the estimated probability that the event will not occur (*not continue*). (Remember, this is a sample, and the probabilities are estimates of the population probabilities.)

Probabilities are one way to express the likelihood of events. As seen from Table 2.1, the probability that one-parent families plan to continue is .4082, and the probability that they do not is .5918($1 - .4082$). The probability that two-parent families plan to continue is .6220, and the probability that they do not is .3780($1 - .6220$).

Odds

The odds are another way to express the likelihood that an event will occur. Sometimes in day-to-day language, we use the term "odds" to refer to probabilities (e.g., the probability that someone plans to continue fostering), but that is not what we mean here. The odds is a *ratio of probabilities*. More specifically, the **odds** is a ratio of the probability that some event will occur to the probability that it will not occur. We can calculate the odds of continuation for one- and two-parent families as follows:

$$\text{odds} = \frac{\hat{p}}{1 - \hat{p}}$$

In our example, the odds of continuation for one-parent families are 0.69 (0.4082/0.5918). The odds of continuation for two-parent families are 1.65 (0.6220/0.3780).

Unlike probabilities, which can only range from 0 to 1, odds can range from 0 to positive infinity, theoretically, and a value of 1 indicates that both outcomes are equally likely. Table 2.2 illustrates the relationship between probabilities and odds. When $\hat{p} = .50$ (both outcomes are equally likely), the odds equal 1. As you see, as $\hat{p}$ increases the odds increase, but *not by a constant amount*. For example, when $\hat{p}$ goes from .70 to .80 the odds increase from 2.33 to 4.00, but when $\hat{p}$ goes from .80 to .90 the odds increase from 4.00 to 9.00.

Odds Ratios

Since our interest is whether two-parent families are more likely to continue fostering than one-parent families, it is useful to compare the odds of continuing for different values of the IV (one- and two-parent families). The odds of continuing for two-parent families are more than double the odds for one-parent families. More specifically, the ratio of these two odds, the **odds ratio (OR)**, is: $1.6455/0.6898 = 2.39$. The OR plays an important role in quantifying the strength and direction of relationships between IVs and DVs in binary, multinomial, and ordinal logistic regression, so we will spend some time here considering its properties.

The OR is the ratio of the odds of the event for one value of the IV (e.g., two-parent families) divided by the odds for a different value of the IV, usually a value one unit lower (e.g., one-parent families). The OR indicates the amount of change in the odds and the direction of the relationship between an IV and DV.

Table 2.2 Probabilities and Corresponding Odds

p	.01	.10	.20	.30	.40	.50	.60	.70	.80	.90	.99
Odds	0.01	0.11	0.25	0.43	0.67	1.00	1.50	2.33	4.00	9.00	99.00

An OR equal to 1 indicates that the odds of the event are the same regardless of the value of the IV; an OR greater than 1 indicates that the odds of the event increase as values of the IV increase (a positive relationship); and an OR less than 1 indicates that the odds of the event decrease as values of the IV increase (a negative relationship). For example, the OR in our example is 2.39, indicating that the odds that two-parent families plan to continue are greater than the odds for one-parent families (1.6455 versus 0.6898). What if the odds were the same for one- and two-parent families (e.g., 1.50 for both)? In that case, the OR would equal 1.00 (i.e., $1.50/1.50 = 1.00$), indicating no difference in the odds for one- and two-parent families, and thus no relationship between marital status and continuation. What if the odds were reversed (i.e., 0.6898 for two-parent families and 1.6455 for one-parent families)? In that case, the OR would be less than 1.00 (i.e., $0.6898/1.6455 = 0.42$).

The size of the OR indicates the amount of change in the odds of the event (e.g., continuation) associated with a change in the IV. For example, in going from one- to two-parent families, the odds of continuing increases by a factor of 2.39 [$2.385 \times 0.6898 = 1.6455$].

The strength and direction of a relationship quantified by the OR can be expressed in different ways. For example, you could express the OR of 2.39 as follows:

- *A one-unit increase in the IV increases the odds of continuing by a factor of 2.39.*
- *The odds of continuing are 2.39 times higher for two-parent compared to one-parent families.*

It would be incorrect to say that *two-parent families are 2.39 times as likely to continue*. This means that the probability that two-parent families plan to continue is 2.39 times higher when in fact it's only 1.45 times higher (i.e., $.5918/.4082 = 1.45$) (DeMaris, 2004).

ORs of less than 1 are a little more difficult to express in words than ORs of greater than 1. Suppose the OR is 0.50. You could express this in different ways:

- *A one-unit increase in the IV decreases the odds of continuing by a factor of .50.*
- *The odds that two-parent families will continue are 0.50 (or one-half) of the odds that one-parent families will continue.*

Another way to express ORs of less than 1 is to compute the *reciprocal* (i.e., 1/OR) and express the relationship in terms of the opposite of the event of interest (i.e., discontinuing instead of continuing). For example, if the OR is 0.50, the reciprocal (1/0.50) is 2.00 and you could say:

- *A one-unit increase in the IV increases the odds of discontinuing by a factor of 2.00.*
- *The odds that two-parent families will discontinue are 2.00 times (or twice) the odds of one-parent families.*

Another especially useful way to express ORs is in terms of *percentage change* in the odds associated with a one-unit increase in the IV. The formula for converting the OR to percentage change is: $100(OR - 1)$. So, in our example, you could say:

- *A one-unit increase in the IV increases the odds of continuing by 139.00% [100(2.39 − 1) = 139.00].*

Or, for example, if the OR is .50 you can say:

- *A one-unit increase in the IV decreases the odds of continuing by 50.00% [100(0.50 − 1) = −50.00].*

Percentage change provides the same information as the OR, and which you use is a matter of preference, but many people find percentage change easier to understand.

In linear regression, it is easy to compare the size of negative and positive slopes—you just ignore the sign and compare the values. For example, a slope of $-.75$ indicates a stronger relationship than a slope of $+.50$. However, to compare the strength of ORs when one OR is less than 1 and the other OR is greater than 1, you need to take the reciprocal (1/OR) of one of the ORs. For example, suppose that you have an OR of 2.00 and an OR of 0.50. The reciprocal of 0.50 is 2.00 $(1/0.50 = 2.00)$, so you would conclude that the ORs are equal in size (but not in the direction of the relationship).

Qualitative descriptors are useful for interpreting and communicating the strength of the relationships between variables. Rosenthal (1996) proposed the guidelines for ORs shown in Table 2.3. (These guidelines have limitations and should be used cautiously.) In particular, the sizes of ORs, like unstandardized regression slopes, depend on how the IVs are

Table 2.3 Qualitative Interpretation of ORs

$OR > 1$	$OR < 1$	Descriptor
1.50	0.67	Weak/small
2.50	0.40	Moderate/medium
4.00	0.25	Strong/large
10.00	0.10	Very strong/very large

measured (Cohen et al., 2003). The relative size of unstandardized regression slopes and ORs cannot be compared for IVs measured on different scales. For example, an OR associated with a one-unit change in marital status is not comparable to an OR associated with a 1-year increase in age.

Finally, most often the odds ratio is abbreviated by OR. Sometimes, for reasons we will discuss below, the odds ratio is symbolized by e^B, $\mathrm{Exp}(B)$, or $\exp(B)$. We will use OR except when discussing hypotheses about the population value of the odds ratio, in which case we will use ψ (psi, pronounced like "sci" in science).

One Dichotomous Independent Variable

Binary Logistic Regression Model

Logits

In linear regression, the estimated value of the DV, usually symbolized as $\hat{Y}$ is the mean of a continuous DV. But in binary logistic regression, the estimated value, L, is the natural logarithm (or simply log) of the odds, typically called the **logit** for short, and it is written as:

$$ ln\left[\frac{\hat{p}}{1 - \hat{p}} \right] $$

In the formula above, $\hat{p}$ is the estimated probability of the outcome (the category coded 1).

The estimated binary logistic regression model for our bivariate example can be written in much the same way as the linear regression model:

$$ L_{(\text{Continue})} = a + B_{\text{Married}}X_{\text{Married}} $$

The right-hand side of this equation looks just like the right-hand side of the linear regression equation. Just as in linear regression, each IV has a slope that indicates the amount of change in the DV associated with a one-unit increase in the IV, controlling for the other IVs. Also, just as in linear regression, the intercept is symbolized by a, each slope is symbolized by B, and each IV is symbolized by X.

As with linear regression, the binary logistic regression equation can be used to compute estimated values for each case, given the values of the IVs for that case. In linear regression, the value estimated by the regression equation is the mean value of the DV. In binary logistic regression, the estimated value is the natural logarithm of the odds that the DV equals 1 (e.g., in our study that the family will continue to foster), the logit.

Estimated values are obtained in binary logistic regression the same way as they are in linear regression: Replace the IVs in the equation with specific values of the IVs (e.g., 0 or 1 for marital status). Then, multiply values of the IVs by their respective slopes, sum the resulting products, and add the intercept. This is similar to computing estimated values of the mean for the continuous DV in linear regression, except that the estimated value is the mean logit.

> What is a *logit* and why do we talk about it? The *logit* is simply the natural logarithm (or *log*) of the odds that the event will occur or that the characteristic is present—the positive of the two possible outcomes. Logits can range from negative to positive infinity, theoretically, and 0 indicates that both outcomes are equally likely. The *logit* has no substantive meaning, and you generally will not discuss it at length. (You will be more likely to talk about the probabilities or the odds of the positive outcome.). However, estimated logits are useful for examining curvilinear relationships and interaction effects, which we discuss later in this chapter, and in computing odds, ORs, and probabilities.

Table 2.4 shows partial results of the binary logistic regression with marital status as the IV and continuation as the DV. For one-parent families, the estimated logit equals:

$$L_{(\text{Continue})} = -.372 = -.372 + (.869)(0)$$

Table 2.4 Parameter Estimates

Parameter	B	Std. Error	95% Wald CI		Hypothesis Test			Exp(B)	95% Wald CI Exp(B)	
			Lower	Upper	Wald Chi-Square	df	Sig.		Lower	Upper
(Intercept)	−.372	.2907	−.941	0.198	1.634	1	.201	0.690	0.390	1.219
[Married = 1]	.869	.3693	.146	1.593	5.544	1	.019	2.385	1.157	4.919
[Married = 0]	0[a]							1		
(Scale)	1[b]									

[a] Set to zero because this parameter is redundant.
[b] Fixed at the displayed value.

For two-parent families, the estimated logit equals:

$$L_{(\text{Continue})} = .497 = -.372 + (.869)\,(1)$$

The number of parameters estimated for a categorical IV is m − 1, where m is the number of categories. So, in Table 2.4 only one set of parameters is estimated and reported for *Married*. We will delete this line of information from subsequent SPSS tables. Also, discussion of modification of the *Scale* parameter shown in Table 2.4 is beyond the scope of this book, and we will delete this line of information from subsequent SPSS tables. See Norusis (2007) for a discussion of this issue.

The relationship between marital status and continuation in terms of logits is illustrated in Figure 2.1. The relationship is positive, and for a one-unit increase in marital status the estimated logit increases from −.37 to .50 by .87, which is the slope, the expected change in the logit associated with a one-unit increase in the IV. A positive slope indicates a positive relationship between the IV and DV; a negative slope indicates a negative relationship; and 0 indicates no linear relationship, just as in linear regression. However, the expected values and the substantive interpretation of the slope have different meanings in binary logistic and linear regression.

In our example, for one-parent families the logit equals −.372 and for two-parent families it is .497. The slope equals .869, and it indicates

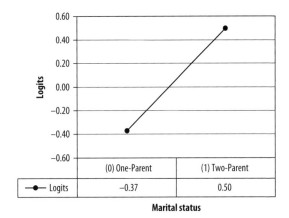

Figure 2.1 Effect of Marital Status on Plans to Continue Fostering (Logits)

the expected change in the logit for a one-unit increase in the IV. The intercept, a, is the estimated value of the logit when the IV equals 0.

Odds

Odds, ORs, and probabilities are key to interpreting results of a binary logistic regression, and they can be easily obtained from the results of a binary logistic regression analysis. You need to know how to do this, and to do it you need to understand and be able to do some relatively simple calculations.

Take the square root of a number; for example, the square root of 4 is 2 ($\sqrt{4} = 2$). To get back to the original number, you just square the square root ($2^2 = 4$). Squaring the number does the reverse of taking the square root; in mathematics this is called an *inverse* function. You need to do something like this to get the odds from the log of the odds (i.e., the logit).

You convert a logit back to the odds by *exponentiation*, that is, raising the base of the natural logarithm to the log of the odds. The exponential function is the inverse of the log function, just as squaring a number is the inverse of taking the square root. On your calculator, it is probably symbolized by e^x, and in SPSS and MS Excel the mathematical function is $\exp(x)$.

For our example, the estimated odds of a dichotomous outcome (e.g., continuing to foster) can be calculated as:

$$\text{odds} = e^{a + B_{\text{Married}} X_{\text{Married}}}$$

That is, the estimated value of the linear predictor ($a + B_{\text{Married}} X_{\text{Married}}$) is exponentiated to get the odds or, equivalently:

$$\text{odds} = e^{L}$$

That is, the estimated value of the logit (L) is exponentiated to get the odds.

For example, in the previous section, we determined that $L = -.372$ for one-parent families, so we exponentiate L to get the odds: $e^{-.372} = .69$. For two-parent families $L = .498$, so the odds that two-parent families will continue are $e^{.498} = 1.65$. **Go ahead and try these**

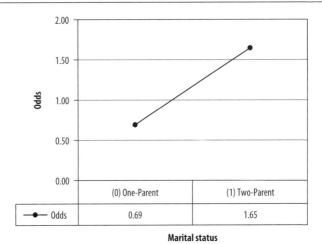

Marital status

Figure 2.2 Effect of Marital Status on Plans to Continue Fostering (Odds)

calculations now using your calculator, SPSS, or MS Excel to make sure that you can exponentiate a logit.

The relationship between marital status and continuation in terms of odds is illustrated in Figure 2.2. The relationship is positive, and for a one-unit increase in marital status the estimated odds increase from 0.69 to 1.65. Compare this to Figure 2.1 above, and note that as the log of the odds (the logit) increases, the odds also increase.

Odds Ratios

Once you know the odds for each value of the IV, you simply take the ratio of one to the other to get the OR. As illustrated above in Figure 2.2, for a one-unit increase in marital status (i.e., one-parent to two-parent families) the estimated odds increase from 0.69 to 1.65, so the OR equals 2.39 (1.65/0.69).

The OR for an IV also can be calculated by exponentiating the associated slope. The slope for marital status, as shown above in Table 2.4, is .869. So, the OR = $2.38 = e^{.869}$. Note in Table 2.4 that this is reported as part of the SPSS output, labeled "Exp(B)." The slope and the OR, then, are closely related and, more specifically, when $B = 0, OR = 1$; when $B < 0, OR < 1$; and when $B > 0, OR > 1$.

Probabilities

The binary logistic model also can be expressed in terms of probabilities (the "inverse link function" referred to in Chapter 1):

$$\hat{p}_{(\text{Continue})} = \frac{e^L}{1 + e^L}$$

(Since the odds $= e^L$, another way to express this is:

$$\hat{p}_{(\text{Continue})} = \frac{\text{odds}}{1 + \text{odds}}$$

Sometimes this formula is written as:

$$\hat{p}_{(\text{Continue})} = \frac{1}{1 + e^{-L}}$$

So, the estimated probability of continuation, $\hat{p}_{(\text{Continue})}$ can be calculated from L, the estimated logit. This is similar to computing estimated values of the mean for the DV in linear regression for cases with different characteristics, except here we are estimating the mean probability. In our example, the estimated probability that one-parent families plan to continue is expressed as:

$$\hat{p}_{(\text{Continue})} = \frac{e^{-.3716}}{1 + e^{-.3716}} = \frac{.6896}{1.6896} = .4082$$

The estimated probability that two-parent families plan to continue is expressed as:

$$\hat{p}_{(\text{Continue})} = \frac{e^{.4978}}{1 + e^{.4978}} = \frac{1.6451}{2.6451} = .6220$$

The relationship between marital status and continuation in terms of probabilities is illustrated in Figure 2.3. The relationship is positive, and for a one-unit increase in marital status the estimated probability increases from .41 to .62. Compare this to Figure 2.1 above, and note that as the log of the odds (logit) increases, the probabilities also increase.

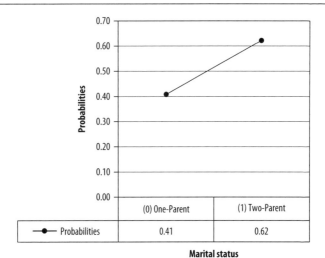

Figure 2.3 Effect of Marital Status on Plans to Continue Fostering (Probabilities)

One Quantitative Independent Variable

Binary Logistic Regression Model

The use and interpretation of binary logistic regression are much the same with quantitative and categorical IVs. We start with a simple example to illustrate the use of binary logistic regression with a quantitative IV. The research question is this: *Are foster families with more resources more likely to continue fostering?*

Table 2.5 shows partial results of this regression analysis. The slope (.212) is positive, and the OR (1.237) is greater than 1, indicating a positive relationship between number of resources and foster continuation.

Logits

We computed the estimated logit for 1 through 11 resources using the following regression equation:

$$L_{(\text{Continue})} = -1.227 + (.212)(X)$$

There were no families with 0 resources, so in a way the intercept is hypothetical and 0 resources has little meaning as a reference point.

Table 2.5 Parameter Estimates

Parameter	B	Std. Error	95% Wald CI		Hypothesis Test				95% Wald CI Exp(B)	
			Lower	Upper	Wald Chi-Square	df	Sig.	Exp(B)	Lower	Upper
(Intercept)	−1.227	.6517	−2.504	0.050	3.544	1	.060	0.293	0.082	1.052
Resources	.212	.0957	0.025	0.400	4.924	1	.026	1.237	1.025	1.492

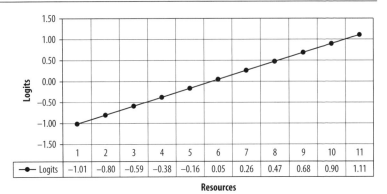

Figure 2.4 Effect of Resources on Plans to Continue Fostering (Logits)

The relationship between resources and continuation in terms of logits is illustrated in Figure 2.4. The relationship is positive, and for a one-unit increase in resources (i.e., one resource in this case) the estimated logit increases by .21 (i.e., the slope). Like the linear regression coefficient, the slope in binary logistic regression can be interpreted as the change in the DV, in this case the logit, associated with a one-unit increase in the IV.

Odds

Remember that the logit, the slope, and the intercept from a binary logistic regression have no intuitive or substantive meaning, although the slope does indicate the direction of the relationship. The computation and meaning of each of these terms are equivalent in the one-quantitative-variable model and the one-categorical-variable model we discussed above. Therefore, we computed the estimated odds of continuing for 1 through 11 resources, using the estimated logits illustrated in Figure 2.4. The estimated odds of continuation for each value of *Resources* were calculated using the formula: e^L, where L was the estimated logit. For example, for one resource the estimated logit equals -1.01, and, using exponentiation, we see that the estimated odds equals 0.36 (i.e., $e^{-1.10} = 0.36$).

The relationship between resources and foster continuation in terms of odds is illustrated in Figure 2.5. You can see the positive relationship between *Resources* and *Continuation*. The odds of continuing range from 0.36 for families with one resource to 3.03 for families with 11 resources.

Notice again that the relationship between resources and odds is not linear. (Remember that in binary logistic regression, the relationship between IVs and logits is linear, but the relationship between IVs and odds is not.) That is, the change in the odds is different depending on the initial value of resources. For example, in going from one to two resources the odds increase from 0.36 to 0.45 (0.09), and in going from 10 to 11 resources the odds increase from 2.45 to 3.03 (0.58). (You can see how important this kind of information could be to foster care agencies, as they look at the resources that potential foster families bring to the table.)

Certainly this lack of a linear relationship between the IV and the DV means that in binary logistic regression the examination and presentation of the relationships between the IVs and the changes in odds are somewhat complicated with multiple IVs.

Odds Ratios

One useful feature of a graph such as Figure 2.5 is that it is possible to easily determine the OR associated with any amount of change in an IV, not just a one-unit increase. That is, instead of the change in the odds associated with each additional family resource, you could examine the change in the odds associated with more than one additional family

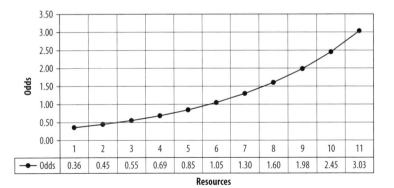

	1	2	3	4	5	6	7	8	9	10	11
Odds	0.36	0.45	0.55	0.69	0.85	1.05	1.30	1.60	1.98	2.45	3.03

Resources

Figure 2.5 Effect of Resources on Plans to Continue Fostering (Odds)

resource. For example, the OR associated with an increase of four family resources equals 2.36 (0.85 / 0.36). In general, though, the OR for any unit of change can be calculated for an IV by first multiplying the slope by the unit of change (e.g., 4), and then exponentiating this value. For example, the slope for resources equals .212, .212 × 4 equals 0.848, and $e^{.848} = 2.34$. (The values of 2.34 and 2.36 are different because of rounding error.)

Probabilities

We also computed the estimated probability of continuing for 1 through 11 resources, using the estimated logits illustrated in Figure 2.4. Each estimated probability was calculated using the formula discussed above:

$$\hat{p}_{\text{(Continue)}} = \frac{e^L}{1 + e^L}$$

For example, for one resource the estimated probability is:

$$.27 = \frac{e^{-1.01}}{1 + e^{-1.01}}$$

The relationship between resources and continuation in terms of probabilities is illustrated in Figure 2.6, and as you can see, it is positive. The probability of continuing ranges from .27 for families with one resource to .75 for families with 11 resources.

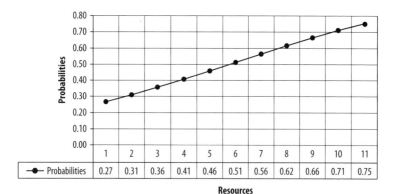

	1	2	3	4	5	6	7	8	9	10	11
—●— Probabilities	0.27	0.31	0.36	0.41	0.46	0.51	0.56	0.62	0.66	0.71	0.75

Resources

Figure 2.6 Effect of Resources on Plans to Continue Fostering (Probabilities)

Notice that the change in the probabilities differs, depending on the initial value of resources. That is, the relationship between resources and probabilities is not linear, and it cannot be linear because a probability cannot be greater than 1. However, in this example, the lack of linearity is not as obvious as is sometimes the case. For example, in going from one to two resources, the probability increases from .27 to .31 (.04), and from seven to eight resources, the probability increases from .56 to .62 (.06). (This is consistent, of course with our findings using the OR, above.) Again, examining and presenting the relationship between IVs and change in the probability of the outcome is not complicated with a single IV, as you see here, but it can be a bit more complicated with multiple IVs.

Scaling Quantitative Independent Variables

The binary logistic regression slope is analogous to the unstandardized linear regression slope in the sense that the size of the slope depends on the scale of the IV. The same is true for the OR.

The size of the OR indicates the amount of change in the odds of the event (e.g., continuation) associated with a one-unit increase in the IV. ORs can be deceptively small for quantitative variables that can take on a large number of values within the limits of the variable. For example, suppose that one study measured the effect of maternal depression on continuation, and depression was measured on a 5-point ordinal scale. Suppose that a second study examined the same question, but measured depression using a standardized scale with a potential range of values from 1 through 100. If the strength of the relationship between depression and continuation were exactly the same in both studies, the OR would be much smaller when depression was measured on a scale from 1 through 100 simply because of the difference in how "one unit" was defined (i.e., one-fifth versus one-hundredth of the scale width). Or, if the strength of the relationship between depression and continuation were actually much stronger in the second study, the OR in the second study could be much smaller than the OR in the first study because of the difference in how "one unit" was defined.

Before including a quantitative IV in a binary logistic regression analysis, you should give some thought to how the variable is scaled and if it might be best to rescale it to make it easier to use or interpret. For example, suppose you measured the variable *income* in units of $1,000 per year, so a family whose annual income was $50,000 would have a value of 50. It might be more meaningful to examine the effect of yearly income in units of $10,000 instead of $1,000. One way you could do this is to compute a new variable, *income* divided by 10, and use this rescaled *income* variable in your analysis. (Our example family would thus have a value of 5 on the rescaled variable.) In doing this, you change the meaning of "one unit" of yearly income from $1,000 to $10,000 (i.e., by a factor of 10).

Factor Change

The OR for a one-unit change in the value of the IV may not be the most meaningful unit, as with our income example. Fortunately, ORs for any incremental change in an IV can be computed by multiplying the slope by some factor, c, and exponentiating this value: $e^{(B)(c)}$. For example, the slope for number of resources is .212, and the OR associated with an increase of two resources equals $1.53(e^{(.212)(2)})$. (Note: first multiply the slope by 2, and then exponentiate.)

Standard (z) Scores

Both unstandardized and standardized slopes are available with linear regression, and both indicate the expected change in the DV associated with a one-unit increase in the IV. The difference is in the units used to quantify the IV and the DV.

Unstandardized linear regression slopes are based on the original units used to measure the IV and DV (e.g., number of resources, income in thousands of dollars per year). Standardized linear regression slopes, in contrast, are based on **standard scores**, also called "z-scores." Standard scores always have a mean of zero and a standard deviation of 1. A z-score indicates how far and in what direction the value of a score deviates from the distribution's mean. So, a one-unit increase in the IV refers to a one standard-deviation increase in the IV, whatever the standard deviation may be for that IV. (You should find out what the standard deviation is from your descriptive statistics.)

Counterparts of standardized slopes for linear regression have been developed for binary logistic regression (Hardin & Hilbe, 2007; Pampel, 2000), but they are not widely used and they are not included in SPSS output. However, you can transform your quantitative IVs to standard scores, and then analyze the standard scores for the IVs, and this can be useful at times. Unlike in linear regression, only the IV (*not* the DV) is in standard scores in this case—this is why the resulting slopes sometimes are called *semi-standardized* slopes.

The formula for transforming a variable to z-scores is:

$$X_{(z)} = \frac{X - M}{SD}$$

where X is the IV score for a case, M is the mean for the IV, and SD is the standard deviation for the IV. In our example, $M = 6.60$, $SD = 1.93$. To create a new variable, *zResources,* for each case, subtract 6.60 from the number of resources, and divide this value by 1.93.

Again, the mean of a variable transformed to standard scores will always be 0, values above the mean will be positive, and values below the mean will be negative. (When you transform a variable to standard scores, the resulting variable is rescaled to standard-deviation units in place of the original units.) So, for example, a value of +1 will correspond to a value one standard deviation above the mean, a value of -1 will correspond to a value one standard deviation below the mean, and a one-unit increase in the IV will correspond to a one standard-deviation increase.

Transforming a variable to standard scores will change its intercept, slope, and OR, but not the associated test statistics from the binary logistic regression. The slope for a variable transformed to standard scores is interpreted as expected change in the logit associated with a one standard-deviation increase in the IV, and the OR is interpreted as the change in the odds associated with a one standard-deviation increase in the IV.

We transformed resources to z-scores to illustrate interpretation of binary logistic regression results with a standardized variable. Table 2.6 shows partial results of the binary logistic regression with *zResources.*

Compare results in Table 2.6 to those above in Table 2.5 for *Resources.* In particular, notice that with *zResources* the slopes and ORs are different because in this analysis "a one-unit increase" refers to an increase of one standard deviation (1.93 resources in this example). Therefore, the OR for *zResources* indicates the change in the odds associated with a one

Table 2.6 Parameter Estimates

| Parameter | B | Std. Error | 95% Wald CI | | Hypothesis Test | | | Exp(B) | 95% Wald CI Exp(B) | |
			Lower	Upper	Wald Chi-Square	df	Sig.		Lower	Upper
(Intercept)	.174	.1789	-.177	0.525	0.947	1	.330	1.190	0.838	1.690
zResources	.410	.1846	.048	0.771	4.924	1	.026	1.506	1.049	2.163

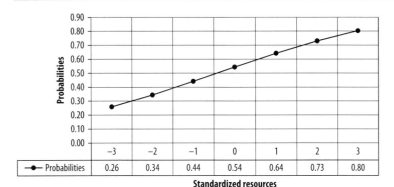

Figure 2.7 Effect of Standardized Resources on Plans to Continue Fostering (Probabilities)

standard-deviation (1.93) increase in resources, not an increase of one resource.

Figure 2.7 shows the relationship between *zResources* and estimated probabilities for this analysis. Compare results in Figure 2.7 to those above in Figure 2.6 for *Resources*. In Figure 2.7, 0 represents the mean number of resources, −1, −2, and −3 indicate the number of standard deviations below the mean, and 1, 2, and 3 indicate the number of standard deviations above the mean. So, for example, the estimated probability of continuing is .54 for families with the mean number of resources (6.60), .34 for families with resources two standard deviations below the mean [6.60−(2 × 1.93)] = 2.74 resources], and .73 for families with resources two standard deviations above the mean [6.60+(2 × 1.93) = 10.46 resources].

Centering

Similar to standardizing scores, we can also center scores on a certain value. Often, we center scores on the mean, and in fact that is what we are doing with standardization, except in that case we also divide by the *SD*. Centering is useful when testing curvilinear relationships and interaction effects (Cohen et al., 2003), as we illustrate below. Centering can also be useful when a variable has no meaningful zero point (Cohen et al., 2003). For example, no case had zero resources in our example, and so centering at the mean results in a meaningful value of 0 (i.e., cases at the mean).

Below, we center values on the mean. However, this is not the only or always the most meaningful way to center an IV. IVs can be centered on other values. For example, if you use a scale with a clinical cutting score it can be useful to center on that value. Then, positive values will be those above the clinical cutting score, and negative values will be below.

The formula for centering a variable is:

$$X_{(centered)} = X - M$$

where X is the value of the IV for a case, and M is the mean for the IV. (Again, you can see that centering on the mean is similar to converting to a z-score except that you do not divide by the SD.) In our example, $M = 6.60$ and we subtract it from the number of resources for each case to create a new variable, *cResources*. You can create this new variable in SPSS using a compute statement, after first computing the mean.

The mean of a centered variable will be 0, values above the mean will be positive, and values below the mean negative. A centered variable will have the same slope, OR, and associated test statistics as the original IV on which it was based. Centering does change the intercept, though, because the intercept is the estimated value of the DV when the IV equals 0 and with a centered variable 0 representing the mean.

We centered resources to illustrate interpretation of binary logistic regression results with a centered variable. Table 2.7 shows partial results of the binary logistic regression with *cResources*.

Compare results in Table 2.7 to those above in Table 2.5 for *Resources*. The only differences are for the intercept, which now represents the estimated logit when the number of resources equals 0 (0 being the mean number of resources, *not* the number of resources).

Figure 2.8 shows the relationship between *cResources* and estimated probabilities for this analysis. Compare results in Figure 2.8 to the comparable figures above for *Resources* and *zResources*. In Figure 2.8, the number of resources is represented on the horizontal axis; 0 represents the mean number of resources, negative values indicate the number of resources below the mean, and positive values indicate the number of resources above the mean. So, for example, the estimated probability of continuing is .54 for families with the mean number of resources (6.60),

Table 2.7 Parameter Estimates

Parameter	B	Std. Error	95% Wald CI		Hypothesis Test			Exp(B)	95% Wald CI Exp(B)	
			Lower	Upper	Wald Chi-Square	df	Sig.		Lower	Upper
(Intercept)	.174	.1789	−.177	.525	0.947	1	.330	1.190	0.838	1.690
cResources	.212	.0957	.025	.400	4.924	1	.026	1.237	1.025	1.492

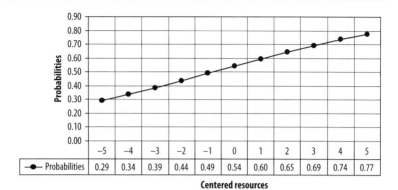

Figure 2.8 Effect of Centered Resources on Plans to Continue Fostering (Probabilities)

.39 for families with 3 resources below the mean $(6.60 - 3 = 3.60)$, and .69 for families with 3 resources above the mean $(6.60 + 3 = 9.60)$.

Logits, Odds, Odds Ratios, and Probabilities Revisited

Suppose you have a single quantitative IV transformed to standard scores, so the mean equals 0 and the standard deviation equals 1. Suppose that the estimated binary logistic regression equation is:

$$L = 0 + (1)(X)$$

Table 2.8 shows values of the IV ranging from three standard deviations below the mean to three above, and the corresponding estimated values of the logit, odds, and probabilities. Notice that when the logit equals 0, the odds equals 1.00, and the probability equals .50. Also, notice that probabilities of less than .50 are associated with odds of less than 1.00 and logits of less than 0. Conversely, probabilities greater than .50 are associated with odds greater than 1.00 and logits greater than 0. Finally, notice that for each one-unit increase in the IV, the ratio of the odds increases by a constant, 2.72 (e.g., 2.72/1.00); this is the OR, the change in the odds associated with a one-unit increase in X. (Notice that we incremented values of X by 0.50, not 1.00.). When you exponentiate the slope, you get the same value (e.g., $e^1 = 2.72$).

Figures 2.9, 2.10, and 2.11 show the relationship between the IV and the estimated logit, odds, and probabilities, respectively. As shown in

Table 2.8 Logits, Odds, and Probabilities as a Function of X

X	logit	odds	p
−3.00	−3.00	.05	.05
−2.50	−2.50	.08	.08
−2.00	−2.00	.14	.12
−1.50	−1.50	.22	.18
−1.00	−1.00	.37	.27
−.50	−.50	.61	.38
.00	.00	1.00	.50
.50	.50	1.65	.62
1.00	1.00	2.72	.73
1.50	1.50	4.48	.82
2.00	2.00	7.39	.88
2.50	2.50	12.18	.92
3.00	3.00	20.09	.95

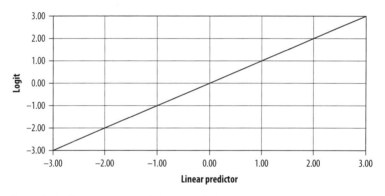

Figure 2.9 Logit as a Function of Linear Predictor

Figure 2.9, the relationship between the IV and the estimated logits is linear, so you can say that a one-unit increase in the IV is associated with a constant change in the logits. The relationships between the IV and the odds and between the IV and the probabilities are not linear, so you cannot say that a one-unit increase in the IV is associated with a constant change in the odds or probabilities. In particular, you see in Figure 2.11 (this figure illustrates the *logistic function* also called the *logistic curve*) that the change associated with a one-unit change in the IV at the lower and upper values of the IV is markedly less than at values closer to the center.

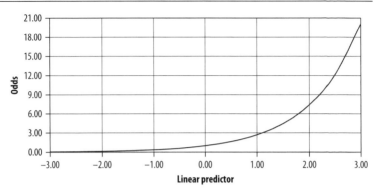

Figure 2.10 Odds as a Function of Linear Predictor

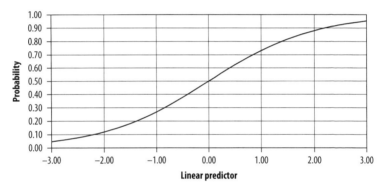

Figure 2.11 Probability as a Function of Linear Predictor

Finally, given that the relationship between the IV and the logit is linear, the relationships between the logit and the odds and between the logit and the probabilities are not linear.

Multiple Independent Variables

In multiple linear regression, the slope indicates expected change in the DV, controlling for other IVs. The same is true in multiple binary logistic regression, except that expected change in the DV refers to change in the logit. More useful in multiple binary logistic regression is the fact that the OR indicates change in the odds associated with a one-unit increase in an IV, controlling for the other IVs (Hardin & Hilbe, 2007). It is also possible to examine expected change in the odds and probabilities of the outcome associated with an increase in an IV, controlling for other IVs, but as we have said before, such relationships aren't linear and so they are a bit more complicated.

Binary Logistic Regression Model

Let us build on our previous two examples in this chapter to illustrate multiple binary logistic regression. Earlier, we saw that families with more resources are more likely to continue fostering, but it is possible that the relationship between family resources and continuation is due to the fact that both are influenced by marital status (i.e., marital status is a *common cause* of both, and so the relationship is *spurious*). So, the research question examined here is this: *Are foster families with more resources more likely to continue fostering, controlling for marital status?* Family resources and marital status are the IVs, and continuation is the DV. The coding for these variables was described above, and we will use *zResources*, although untransformed or centered resources could also be used with the same substantive results.

We know the direction and strength of the relationship between resources and continuation from our previous analyses (see Table 2.6). Now, though, we will enter both *zResources* and marital status into our regression analysis and focus on the change in the relationship between *zResources* and continuation when controlling for marital status. Table 2.9 contains partial results of this analysis.

Without controlling for marital status, the OR for *zResources* is 1.51 (see Table 2.6). Controlling for marital status the OR for *zResources* is 1.26. The smaller value of *zResources* when controlling for marital status implies that marital status may be, at least in part, a common cause of family resources and continuation. (Of course, we could think about this in the opposite way by thinking about resources as the cause of both marital status and continuation. Then, we would be looking at the effects of marital status, controlling for resources. This choice depends upon your knowledge of the substantive area.)

To better understand and present substantive findings, we compute estimated odds, ORs, and probabilities at substantively informative values (e.g., mean number of resources) and for substantively important types of cases (e.g., two-parent families with the mean number of

Table 2.9 Parameter Estimates

| Parameter | B | Std. Error | 95% Wald CI | | Hypothesis Test | | | Exp(B) | 95% Wald CI Exp(B) | |
			Lower	Upper	Wald Chi-Square	df	Sig.		Lower	Upper
(Intercept)	−.183	.3505	−.870	0.504	.273	1	.601	.833	0.419	1.655
zResources	.228	.2389	−.240	0.696	.912	1	.340	1.256	0.787	2.006
[Married = 1]	.570	.4808	−.372	1.513	1.408	1	.235	1.769	0.689	4.540

resources). Or, for continuous IVs without inherently informative substantive values, you might compute and report estimated probabilities using the mean and one or two standard deviations above and below the mean (or the 25% and 75% percentiles), fixing all other IVs at selected values (Hoffmann, 2004; Long & Freese, 2006). We now discuss how to do this.

Logits

The estimated multiple binary logistic regression in this example is:

$$L_{(Continue)} = -.183 + .228_{zResources}X_{zResources} + .570_{Married}X_{Married}$$

As discussed in our previous examples, estimated values of the logits can be calculated by replacing the Xs with specific values of the IVs (e.g., 0 or 1 for marital status). Estimated logits then can be used to calculate the odds, ORs, and probabilities, which are necessary to fully describe the results of a binary logistic regression. For example, for one-parent families with the mean number of resources (i.e., 0, because we transformed the number of resources into standard scores), the estimated logit would be:

$$-.183 = -.183 + (.228)(0) + (.570)(0)$$

Odds

As discussed in our previous examples, estimated values of the odds of the outcome can be calculated from estimated logits by e^L. For example, L equals $-.183$ for one-parent families with the mean number of resources, so the odds that such families plan to continue are: $e^{-.183} = .83$.

The challenge is to summarize changes in IVs associated with changes in odds in the most meaningful and parsimonious way; however, no standard way to do this exists, and again, it depends partly on your understanding of your substantive area. This is complicated by the fact that the relationships between IVs and odds are not linear. For any given analysis, you should explore different ways to present the key substantive findings in tables or graphs (Long & Freese, 2006).

Odds for cases with different values of the IVs can be presented in tables. Table 2.10 shows estimated odds for one- and two-parent

Table 2.10 Estimated Odds for Marital Status and Family Resources

	Estimated Odds Family Resources		
Marital Status	*M − 2SD*	*M*	*M + 2SD*
One-Parent	0.53	.83	1.31
Two-Parents	0.93	1.47	2.32

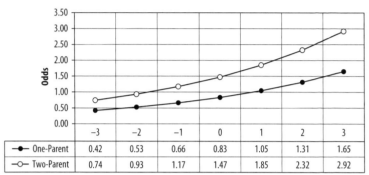

	−3	−2	−1	0	1	2	3
—●— One-Parent	0.42	0.53	0.66	0.83	1.05	1.31	1.65
—○— Two-Parent	0.74	0.93	1.17	1.47	1.85	2.32	2.92

Standardized resources

Figure 2.12 Effect of Resources and Marital Status on Plans to Continue Fostering (Odds)

families with three different levels of family resources. For example, the odds are relatively high that two-parent families with many resources will continue (2.32) and relatively low for one-parent families with few resources (0.53).

Finally, in addition to presenting odds in tables, oftentimes it can be useful to present them in graphic form, such as Figure 2.12, which shows the effect of *zResources* for one- and two-parent families. The larger the number of IVs, though, the more difficult this becomes, and only a limited number of IVs can be represented meaningfully on a single graph. One way to do this is to plot the relationship of one IV from its minimum to maximum value, while all other variables are fixed at their mean (or, for dichotomous variables, 0 or 1). Another strategy is to estimate odds for selected sets of values of IVs that correspond to ideal or typical types in the population (e.g., single-parent families with the mean number of resources) (Long, 1997).

For example, a foster care agency is interested in understanding which families will continue to foster long enough to make the significant investment in recruiting, selecting, training, and supervising those families worthwhile. They want to see whether shaping their recruitment policies will maximize continuation, and will present the findings of their study to the board for consideration of such changes. Clearly, the board will find no meaning in logits, and so the agency may present the findings, for example, in one of the following ways (see Table 2.10 or Figure 2.12):

We found that the odds of continuing to foster for one-parent families with above-average resources (odds = 1.31) were 2.47 (1.31/0.53) times as great as the odds for one-parent families with below-average resources (odds = 0.53); or

We found that the odds of continuing to foster for two-parent families with above-average resources (odds = 2.32) were 4.38 (2.32/0.53) times as great as the odds for one-parent families with below-average resources (odds = 0.53).

Odds Ratios

The OR associated with each IV and reported in the SPSS output as Exp(B) shows the estimated change in the odds of the outcome associated with a one-unit increase in the IV, when controlling for other IVs. These are not necessarily the only meaningful ORs. Other types of comparisons can also be made. For example, consider the information in Table 2.10 and Figure 2.12. You could, for example, compare the odds of continuation for two-parent families with two standard deviations above the mean number of resources (odds = 2.32) to one-parent families with two standard deviations below the mean number of resources (odds = 0.53); the odds of continuation increase by a factor of 4.38 (OR = 4.38 = 2.32/0.53).

Probabilities

The estimated probability of the outcome for cases with the same values of the IVs can be calculated from estimated logits using the following formula discussed earlier:

$$\hat{p}_{(\text{Continue})} = \frac{e^L}{1 + e^L}$$

For example, in the previous section, we determined that L equals $-.183$ for one-parent families with the mean number of resources, so the probability that such families will continue is:

$$\hat{p}_{(\text{Continue})} = \frac{e^{-.183}}{1 + e^{-.183}} = \frac{.833}{1.833} = .46$$

A good place to start looking for the best way to present the probabilities is to examine the frequency distribution of the probabilities for all cases, basic descriptive statistics (e.g., mean, median, standard deviation, range, and interquartile range), and different types of univariate charts (histogram, boxplot, etc.). SPSS will compute expected probabilities for each case. In our current example of one-parent families with the mean number of resources, descriptive statistics for probabilities are as follows: $M = .46$, $Mdn = .42$, $SD = .11$, range $= .29–.67$, and interquartile range $= .37–.56$.

As above, there is no standard way to summarize changes in IVs associated with changes in probabilities in a meaningful way, especially when the relationship between the IVs and the probabilities is not linear. For any given analysis, you should explore different ways to present the key substantive findings in tables or graphs (Long & Freese, 2006). Again, this depends in part on the subject and the objective of the study. For example, previous research in your field may have demonstrated findings in ways that you may want to present your own results.

Probabilities for cases with different values of IVs can be presented in tables. Table 2.11 shows estimated probabilities for one- and two-parent families with three different levels of family resources. For example, two-parent families with many resources are likely to continue, and one-parent families with few resources are not.

In addition to presenting probabilities in tables, often it is useful to present probabilities in graphic form, such as Figure 2.13. The larger the

Table 2.11 Estimated Probabilities for Marital Status and Family Resources

Marital Status	Estimated Probability Family Resources		
	$M - 2SD$	M	$M + 2SD$
One-Parent	.35	.45	.57
Two-Parents	.48	.60	.70

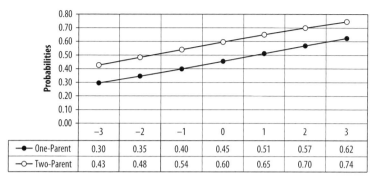

Figure 2.13   Effect of Standardized Resources and Marital Status on Plans to Continue Fostering (Probabilities)

number of IVs though, the more difficult this becomes. Only a limited number of IVs can be represented meaningfully on a single graph.

Comparing the Relative Strength of Independent Variables

In linear regression, the standardized slope is used to compare the relative strength of different IVs. The standardized slope indicates expected change in the DV in standard deviation units, for a one standard-deviation increase in an IV. That is, the IVs and the DV are both transformed to z-scores.

The binary logistic regression slope is analogous to the unstandardized slope in linear regression. Although binary logistic regression approximations to standardized slopes have been developed (Hardin & Hilbe, 2007), they are not in widespread use and are not shown in SPSS output. Neither the slope nor the OR can take the place of the standardized regression slope (Menard, 2001), so it is more difficult to compare the relative strength of IVs measured in different ways. The sizes of the slope and the OR depend on how the IV is measured, just as they do with the unstandardized slope in linear regression. We explained this point above when we discussed transformations for quantitative IVs. However, when IVs are measured the same way (e.g., two dichotomous IVs or two continuous IVs transformed to z-scores) their relative strength can be compared (Pampel, 2000).

Sometimes you need to compare the sizes of ORs indicating negative and positive relationships. To compare the strength of ORs when one is less than 1 and the other is greater than 1, take the reciprocal (1/OR) of one of the ORs. For example, suppose you have an OR of 2.00 and an OR of 0.50. The reciprocal of 0.50 is 2.00 (1/0.50 = 2.00), so you would conclude that the ORs are equal in size, though not in the direction of the relationship. However, this does not mean that the effects of the IVs are comparable, especially if the IVs are measured using different units (e.g., one is dichotomous and the other is measured on a scale from 0 through 100).

Testing Hypotheses

In binary logistic regression, as in linear regression, you need to test the overall null hypothesis that all slopes equal zero (equivalent to the null hypothesis that all ORs equal 1). Also, you will want to test the null hypothesis that the associated slope equals zero for each IV, (equivalent to the null hypothesis that the OR equals 1), and examine 95% confidence intervals associated with each OR. Finally, at times, you will want to test hypotheses about incremental change in your model when additional IVs are added.

Testing the Null Hypothesis that $\beta_1 = \beta_2 = \beta_k = 0$

Up to this point, we have focused on estimating, interpreting, and presenting the slope, odds, OR, and probabilities. In practice, though, before you would do this, you would test the null hypothesis that all slopes equal 0. That is, you would want to know whether a statistically significant relationship exists between the entire set of IVs on the one hand and the DV on the other. If that is not the case, you probably should not test the individual relationships. To illustrate this, we will continue our example with marital status and *zResources* as IVs.

The test of the null hypothesis that $\beta_{\text{Married}} = \beta_{\text{ZResources}} = 0$ is the same as the test of the null hypothesis that $\psi_{\text{Married}} = \psi_{\text{zResources}} = 1$, where ψ is the symbol for the population value of OR. In linear regression, we use the *omnibus F-test* to test the null hypothesis that $\beta_{\text{Married}} = \beta_{\text{zResources}} = 0$. The binary logistic regression counterpart to the omnibus F-test is the *likelihood ratio χ^2 test*, which is shown in Table 2.12 for the model with marital status and *zResources*. As you see, you can reject the null hypothesis that the slopes for both IVs equal 0.

Table 2.12 Omnibus Test

Likelihood Ratio Chi-Square	df	Sig.
6.585	2	.037

Testing the Null Hypotheses that $\beta_k = 0$

If the omnibus null hypothesis that $\beta_{\text{Married}} = \beta_{z\text{Resources}} = 0$ is rejected, typically the next step is to test the two null hypotheses that $\beta_{\text{Married}} = 0$ and $\beta_{z\text{Resources}} = 0$. The test of the null hypothesis that $\beta_{\text{Married}} = 0$, for example, is the same as the test of the null hypothesis that $\psi_{\text{Married}} = 1$. Directional hypotheses also can be tested. The null hypothesis that $\beta_{\text{Married}} \geq 0$ is the same as $\psi_{\text{Married}} \geq 1$, and $\beta_{\text{Married}} \leq 0$ is the same as $\psi_{\text{Married}} \leq 1$.

In binary linear regression, these null hypotheses are tested in much the same way as in linear regression. In linear regression, the t-statistic is used, but in binary logistic regression SPSS reports the Wald statistic, which serves the same purpose. Sometimes this is called the *Wald χ^2 test* since it has a chi-squared distribution (DeMaris, 2004).

Values of the Wald statistic are shown above in Table 2.9 for marital status and *zResources*. The associated two-tailed p-values (i.e., "Sig.") indicate that neither $\beta_{\text{Married}} = 0$ nor $\beta_{z\text{Resources}} = 0$ can be rejected. This is a little surprising, given that $\beta_{\text{Married}} = \beta_{Z\text{Resources}} = 0$ was rejected, but we will have more to say about this below when we discuss multicollinearity.

In general, the likelihood ratio test is better than the Wald statistic for testing null hypotheses for individual slopes; you can see these in Table 2.13. In large samples, both procedures give approximately the same results, but in small or moderate samples different results are

Table 2.13 Tests of Model Effects

	Type III		
Source	Likelihood Ratio Chi-Square	df	Sig.
(Intercept)	.289	1	.591
zResources	.920	1	.338
Married	1.417	1	.234

possible and the likelihood ratio test is preferred (Kleinbaum & Klein, 2002).

Confidence Intervals for Odds Ratios

The 95% confidence interval (CI) for an OR provides a range of values centered on the sample estimate of the OR known to contain the true value of the OR with a given degree of confidence (usually 95%). Also, the CI can be used to test nondirectional hypotheses for the OR, as well as to provide an interval estimate for the population value of the OR. If the 95% confidence interval for the OR contains 1, the null hypothesis cannot be rejected. If the 95% confidence interval does not contain 1, the null can be rejected (see Table 2.9 above).

Comparing Nested Models

A regression model containing only family resources as the IV is said to be **nested** within a model containing family resources and marital status. In general, one regression model is nested within another if it contains a subset of the variables included in the model within which it's nested, and the same cases are analyzed in both models. Sometimes, the more complex model is called the **full** model and the nested model the **reduced model**. A comparison of the full and reduced models allows you to examine whether one or more variable(s) in the full model contribute to the explanation of the DV. For example, see Figure 2.14 below.

In this illustration, we see the full model containing three IVs on the top row. The second row shows three reduced models, each containing two of the IVs from the full model. Finally, on the bottom row, we see six

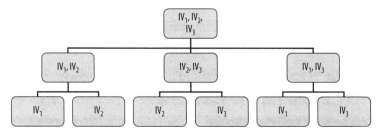

Figure 2.14 Nested Models

models that are further reduced, each containing one of the IVs from the full model.

In regression analyses, we sometimes compare full and reduced models by entering variables sequentially, oftentimes called hierarchical entry. (This is not to be confused with *stepwise* entry, which is something different.) For example, family resources might be entered first in a reduced model to determine if and how it is related to continuation. Then, marital status might be added to make a full model, and the full and reduced models would be compared to determine if and how marital status adds to the explanation of continuation. One reason you might do this is to first determine using the reduced model if family resources is related to continuation and, if it is, to then examine whether this relationship is spurious because family resources and continuation are both caused by marital status (i.e., marital status is a common cause). Another reason you might do this is to see whether marital status makes any additional contribution to explaining continuation, after allowing for family resources. In any case, this sequential entry of IVs is exactly the same as conducting and comparing two separate regression models, one with family resources as the IV, and the other with family resources and marital status—it's just a little easier way of doing it.

In linear regression, you use F_{change} to compare full and reduced models. The binary logistic regression counterpart to F_{change} is the difference between the likelihood ratio χ^2 values for the full and reduced models. (This is true for all of the GZLM models discussed in this book.) Unfortunately, GZLM SPSS does not allow the automatic sequential entry of IVs, so you must estimate and compare full and reduced models.

To illustrate the comparison of full and reduced models, first we estimated a model with *zResources* as the IV, the reduced model [$\chi^2(1) = 5.168$, $p = .023$]. Then, we estimated a model with *zResources* and marital status, the full model [$\chi^2(2) = 6.585, p = .037$]. Next, we subtracted the χ^2 value for the reduced model from the χ^2 value for the full model ($6.585 - 5.168 = 1.417$), and subtracted the degrees of freedom for the reduced model from the degrees of freedom for the full model ($2 - 1 = 1$). Then, we used an Excel file provided on the companion Web site for this book (*Chi-square Difference.xls*) to find that for $\chi^2(1) = 1.417$, $p = .234$. That is, marital status does not add to the explanation of continuation.

Assumptions Necessary for Testing Hypotheses

There are no assumptions unique to binary logistic regression other than the ones we discussed in Chapter 1 (pp. 21–28).

Model Evaluation

As we discussed in Chapter 1, before you test hypotheses or interpret substantive results of any regression model, you should examine how well your regression model fits your data, that is, how effectively the model describes the DV. You will test the overall model, and many times you need to compare different models, as we discussed above. You also need to check for individual cases that are not well explained by the estimated model (i.e., outliers), or that exert undue influence on the estimation of the model. Finally, you will want to know how well your model explains your DV overall. Now, we turn to the specifics of doing this with binary logistic regression.

Outliers

Outliers are data points that are atypical, in that they are markedly different from the other data in the sample. For example, it would be unusual for a one-parent family with virtually no resources to continue fostering. Or, given that the mean number of family resources in our example is 6.60, the standard deviation is 1.93, and the distribution of resources is fairly normal, a family with 20 resources would be unusual indeed. Checking for outliers can help you identify errors and provide insight into how well your regression model fits your data for individual cases.

Outliers can result from data entry or other types of errors (e.g., recording error by an observer), model misspecification (e.g., specifying a relationship as linear when it is curvilinear, or specifying main effects only when interactions are present), rare events (e.g., a 21-year-old with a yearly income of $1,000,000), or numerous other reasons (Cohen et al., 2003). Whatever their cause, outliers can markedly influence the results of your regression analyses (e.g., your slopes and tests of statistical significance) and lead to seriously flawed conclusions, especially in small samples.

On the positive side, outliers can provide theoretical insights. For example, suppose you identified single-parent families with virtually no resources who planned to continue fostering; a careful examination of the other characteristics of these cases might lead to new insights about why some families plan to continue fostering, and this in turn might lead to changes in your regression model (e.g., the addition of variables thought to explain continuation). For example, it might be that single-parent families with virtually no resources who planned to continue fostering were fostering relatives—i.e., providing "kinship care". The inclusion of a dichotomous IV indicating whether or not a family was providing kinship care might result in a better specified regression model.

A data point may be atypical in various ways. The value of an IV may be extremely large or small relative to other values of the IV (e.g., a family with 20 resources). Or the estimated value of the DV for a case may be very different than the actual value; that is, the actual value of the DV for a given case is unusual or unexpected given the values of the IV for that case, and it is not explained well by your regression model (e.g., a one-parent family with no resources who continued fostering). In any case, extreme values may exert undue influence on the estimation of the regression model. (By *undue influence,* we mean that the case is so influential that it causes the model to be less representative of the sample as a whole.)

Leverage

In linear regression, leverage measures how unusual a case is in terms of the values of the IVs in the regression model. Imagine a seesaw; the farther away from the middle you get, the more leverage you have. Cases with greater leverage can exert a disproportionately large influence on regression results. SPSS will compute a leverage value for each case.

We know of no clear benchmarks for leverage values with binary logistic regression. However, **index plots** can be used to identify cases with substantially different leverage values than those of other cases (Cohen et al., 2003). An index plot is a scatter plot with case numbers on the horizontal axis, and leverage values, for example, on the vertical axis. Figure 2.15 shows the index plot for our multiple regression example. As you can see, there may be a few cases that are somewhat different from the others (i.e., the five cases greater than or equal to approximately .05), and these cases might be worth investigating. If unusual cases are identified, you can open the SPSS editor for the scatter plot and select

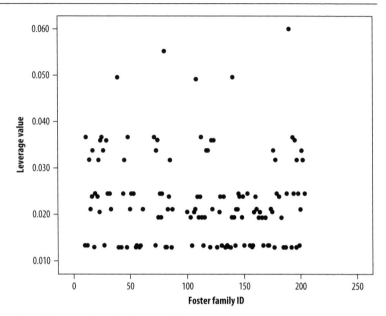

Figure 2.15 Index Plot for Leverage Values

Element/Data Label Mode, and place the cursor over a particular data point to discover the case number for that data point.

Use the following language to get case numbers in SPSS:
Transform > Compute, Sequence = $casenum.

Residuals

A residual is a measure of the difference between the actual and the estimated values of the DV for a case. A large absolute value of a residual indicates a case for which the model fits poorly, and possibly a case that exerts a disproportionately large influence on the estimated regression results. You should not just discard such cases from your analysis; rather, you should examine them and, to the extent that you can, determine why they fit so poorly (Long & Freese, 2006).

With logistic regression, as with linear regression, you can quantify residuals in a number of ways. SPSS computes several different types of residuals for each case. Agreement does not exist on the single best type of residual to examine (e.g., Hardin & Hilbe, 2007; Long & Freese, 2006; Menard, 2001). However, there seems to be some agreement that standardized or unstandardized *deviance residuals* are useful, and SPSS will compute these residuals for each case.

Unlike linear regression, standardized and unstandardized residuals will not be distributed normally, and there are no fixed rules for defining what counts as a large residual (Long & Freese, 2006). Cases that stand out as markedly different certainly warrant investigation. For standardized and unstandardized deviance residuals, values less than -2 or greater than $+2$ also warrant some concern, and values less than -3 or greater than $+3$ merit close inspection (Menard, 2001). Figure 2.16 shows the index plot for our multiple regression example with the standardized deviance residuals on the horizontal axis; no cases have markedly different values from the other cases, and no residual is less than -2 or greater than $+2$.

Influence

Cases whose deletion results in substantial changes to the regression coefficients are said to be influential. **Cook's D** (distance) measures approximate aggregate change in estimated regression parameters resulting from

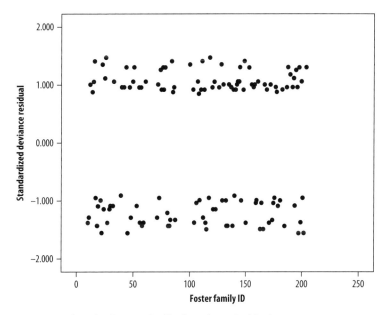

Figure 2.16 Index Plot for Standardized Deviance Residuals

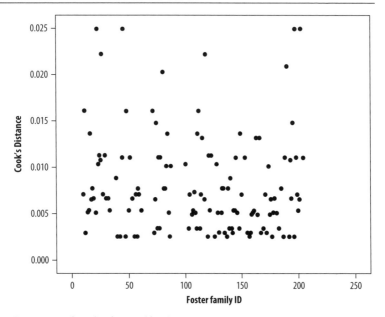

Figure 2.17 Index Plot for Cook's Distance

deletion of a case. SPSS will compute a value of Cook's D for each case. Cohen et al. (2003) and others (Norusis, 2006) note that values of 1.0 or more indicate a problematic degree of influence for an individual case. Other authors suggest much lower cutoffs (Fox, 2008). Figure 2.17 shows the index plot with Cook's D on the vertical axis and case numbers on the horizontal axis; no cases have values of 1.0 or greater. However, there may be a few cases that are somewhat different from the others (i.e., the eight cases greater than or equal to approximately .02), and these cases might be worth investigating.

Summary Measures

Analogs of R^2

In linear regression, R^2 provides a measure of overall model fit, but there is no exact counterpart to the linear regression R^2 in logistic regression. A number of analogs to R^2 exist, but none is in standard use and each may give different results (DeMaris, 2004). Typically, these indices are much smaller than R^2 values in linear regression, and they're difficult to interpret (Norusis, 2006).

Multicollinearity

As discussed in Chapter 1, *multicollinearity* refers to the existence of strong linear relationships among IVs. (The term has nothing to do with your DV.) Multicollinearity occurs when highly related IVs are included in a regression model as, for example, might occur when different measures of the same construct are included in a regression model, or when demographic characteristics are highly correlated.

Multicollinearity should always be examined before interpreting substantive results from any multiple regression analysis. Unfortunately, SPSS does not compute multicollinearity statistics for binary logistic regression. However, since multicollinearity only involves the IVs in a regression model, multicollinearity statistics can be computed using linear regression as described in Chapter 1 (DeMaris, 2004). In our example with two IVs (*zResources* and *Married*), tolerance equals $1 - r^2$, where r^2 is the squared correlation between the two IVs, and $r = .65$. Therefore, tolerance equals .58 and the VIF equals 1.72 (1/.58). Neither of these is near problematic levels (tolerance $< .10$ or VIF > 10).

Additional Topics

Polytomous Independent Variables

You cannot enter multicategorical IVs into a binary regression analysis. Instead, you (or the computer) must create new variables to enter. We will describe the most common method, **dummy (indicator) coding**, but this is only one of many different methods for coding multicategorical IVs (Cohen et al., 2003).

> Whenever dummy-coded or other types of variables are used to represent a multicategorical IV, it is important to remember that all of the variables should be included together as a group. The statistical significance of individual variables should be examined *only* if the group of variables is statistically significant (Menard, 2001)

Dummy (Indicator) Coding

Dummy coding (also called "indicator" coding because it "indicates" the presence or absence of a categorical attribute) is often used in linear regression to code multicategorical IVs. In linear regression, dummy coding contrasts the mean of a reference group with the mean of each remaining category of the categorical IV. In binary logistic regression, the odds of the groups are contrasted using the OR.

In the above example, in which we examined the effect of marital status on continuation while controlling for *zResources*, two-parent families (coded 1) were compared to one-parent families (coded 0). That is, one-parent families were the reference group against which two-parent families were compared. The resulting OR indicated that the odds of continuing were 1.77 higher for two-parent families compared to one-parent families, when controlling for family resources. Alternatively, you could say that the odds of continuing increased by 1.77 for a one-unit increase in the IV (i.e., 0–1 in this example).

Let us extend this example to an IV with more than two categories, although in a way the only difference is that there are more than two categories to be compared to the reference category. Suppose we are interested in whether foster families in one county are less likely to continue fostering than those in two other counties. More specifically, suppose we hypothesize that one county, Davidson, is having an especially difficult time with foster family retention compared to the remaining two counties, Hamilton and Knox. So, the IV is county, which has three categories (Davidson $= 0$, Hamilton $= 1$, and Knox $= 2$), and Davidson county is the reference group against which the other two counties are compared. You can see partial results of the binary logistic regression analysis with these two IVs in Tables 2.14 and 2.15.

The likelihood ratio χ^2 test in Table 2.14 provides an overall test of the null hypothesis that the slopes for the set of county variables equal 0 (or that ORs $= 1$); the associated p value (0.220) indicates that this null hypothesis cannot be rejected. Typically, then you would not interpret the ORs for the county variables, but we'll go ahead and do this to illustrate how the ORs are interpreted. The OR for Hamilton county equals 1.190, indicating that the odds of continuing in Hamilton

Table 2.14 Tests of Model Effects

Source	Type III Likelihood Ratio Chi-Square	df	Sig.
(Intercept)	.287	1	.592
County	3.029	2	.220

Table 2.15 Parameter Estimates

| Parameter | B | Std. Error | 95% Wald CI | | Hypothesis Test | | | Exp(B) | 95% Wald CI Exp(B) | |
			Lower	Upper	Wald Chi-Square	df	Sig.		Lower	Upper
(Intercept)	−.174	.2960	−.755	0.406	.347	1	.556	0.840	0.470	1.501
[County = 2]	.660	.3936	−.112	1.431	2.810	1	.094	1.935	0.894	4.184
[County = 1]	.174	.5191	−.843	1.192	.113	1	.737	1.190	0.430	3.293
[County = 0]	0[a]							1		

[a] Set to zero because this parameter is redundant.

county are 1.190 times higher than in the reference group (Davidson county). The OR for Knox county equals 1.935, indicating that the odds of continuing in Knox county are 1.935 times higher than in the reference group (Davidson county). Note, however, that neither OR is statistically significant. (This is consistent with our findings above that we cannot reject the overall null hypothesis.)

A cross-tabulation of county and foster continuation might also help you understand ORs for multicategorical IVs. This cross-tabulation is in Table 2.16. The OR for Hamilton county is computed as follows: $(0.500/0.500)/(0.457/0.543) = 1.19$. The OR for Knox county is computed as follows: $(0.619/0.381)/(0.457/0.543) = 1.93$. (If you have questions about these computations refer back to the cross-tabulation table and the associated discussion at the beginning of this chapter.)

Curvilinear Relationships

One assumption of binary logistic regression is that the relationship between the linear combination of IVs and the logit is linear. More generally, as discussed in Chapter 1, the relationship between $g(\mu)$ and η is assumed to be linear in the regression models discussed in this book.

Several different methods may be used to test for curvilinearity with binary logistic regression (DeMaris, 2004; Hosmer & Lemeshow, 2000; Norusis, 2006), and oftentimes the inclusion of nonlinear terms is of theoretical interest. For example, suppose we hypothesize that the number of family resources positively influences continuation, but only up to a certain point, beyond which the number of resources has no additional

Table 2.16 Plan to Continue Fostering as a Function of County of Residence

			County			
			(0) Davidson	(1) Hamilton	(2) Knox	Total
Continue Fostering	(0) Not Continue	Count	25	11	24	60
		% within County	54.35	50.00	38.10	45.80
	(1) Continue	Count	21	11	39	71
		% within County	45.65	50.00	61.90	54.20
Total		Count	46	22	63	131
		% within County	100.00	100.00	100.00	100.00

effect. (You might think of this as a threshold relationship—for example, as long as you have the average number of resources, adding more does not increase your probability of continuing.) This is an example of what is known as a *quadratic relationship*. You test this relationship in much the same way you would with linear regression (DeMaris, 2004; Hosmer & Lemeshow, 2000). That is, create and enter two new variables into the regression equation: (1) number of resources centered (*cResources*); and (2) number of resources centered and squared (*cResources*^{2}). If *cResources*^{2} is statistically significant, you would conclude that a curvilinear (quadratic) relationship exists, and you would describe the form of this relationship. If not, reestimate the model without this curvilinear term and interpret results of the "reduced" model.

Results of this analysis (not shown) indicate that *cResources*^{2} is not statistically significant. If it were statistically significant, a useful way to understand and depict the form of the relationship would be to create a graph with *cResources* on the horizontal axis and estimated values of the logit, odds, or probabilities on the vertical axis. As shown in Figure 2.18 (in terms of logits), the number of resources has a positive relationship with continuation up to about one or two resources above the mean (0 on the scatter plot, corresponding to 6.60 resources), and then the direction of the relationship is reversed.

Figures 2.19 and 2.20 indicate essentially the same relationship as Figure 2.18, but odds and probabilities are more easily interpreted and understood. For example, the odds of continuing increase by a factor

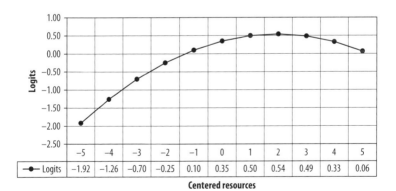

Figure 2.18 Curvilinear Relationship between Centered Resources and Plans to Continue Fostering (Logits)

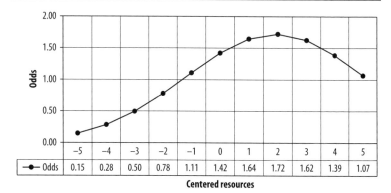

Figure 2.19 Curvilinear Relationship between Centered Resources and Plans to Continue Fostering (Odds)

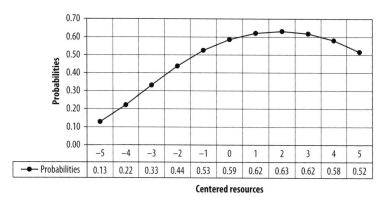

Figure 2.20 Curvilinear Relationship between Centered Resources and Plans to Continue Fostering (Probabilities)

of 2.21 in going from two resources below the mean to two above (i.e., OR = 2.21 = 1.72/0.78) (although if the relationship is curvilinear, the OR will not be constant across different values of the IV). The corresponding probability of continuing goes from .44 to .63 as shown in Figure 2.20.

Interactions

As discussed in Chapter 1, an interaction occurs when the effect of one IV (*focal* variable) is conditional on the values of one or more other IVs (*moderator* variables). The focal variable is the IV whose effect on the DV is thought to vary as a function of the moderator variable.

You test interactions in binary logistic regression in much the same way you do in linear regression, but they are a bit more work to present and interpret, given the nonlinear relationship between the IVs and the odds and probabilities (Jaccard, 2001). For example, suppose you hypothesize that the effect of resources (the *focal* variable) is different for one- and two-parent families (marital status is the *moderator* variable). It may be that resources have a relatively large influence on continuation for one-parent families, but less of an effect for two-parent families. To test this possibility, create and enter two new variables into the regression equation: (1) *cResources* (number of resources centered); and (2) *MaritalXcResources* (marital status multiplied by number of resources centered). If *MaritalXcResources* is statistically significant, you would conclude that the effect of resources is moderated by marital status (i.e., these two variables interact), and you would examine the form of this relationship. If not, reestimate the model without this interaction term and interpret results of the "reduced" model.

Results of this analysis (not shown) indicate no statistically significant interaction. However, if the interaction were statistically significant, a useful way to understand and depict the form of the relationship would be to create a scatter plot with resources centered (the focal variable) on the horizontal axis, estimated logits, odds, or probabilities on the vertical axis, and separate lines representing the relationships between number of resources centered and continuation for one- and two-parent families. (See Figures 2.21, 2.22, and 2.23, respectively.) In the absence of an

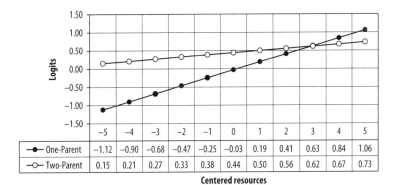

	−5	−4	−3	−2	−1	0	1	2	3	4	5
● One-Parent	−1.12	−0.90	−0.68	−0.47	−0.25	−0.03	0.19	0.41	0.63	0.84	1.06
○ Two-Parent	0.15	0.21	0.27	0.33	0.38	0.44	0.50	0.56	0.62	0.67	0.73

Centered resources

Figure 2.21 Effect of Centered Resources on Plans to Continue Fostering (Logits)

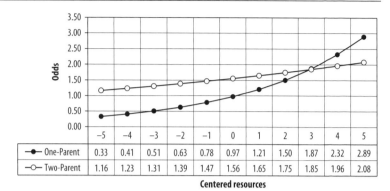

Figure 2.22 Effect of Centered Resources on Plans to Continue Fostering (Odds)

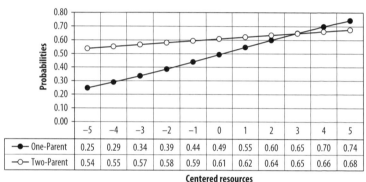

Figure 2.23 Effect of Centered Resources on Plans to Continue Fostering (Probabilities)

interaction, the separate lines for one- and two-parent families will be parallel for the plot of the logits, but not necessarily for the probabilities or odds, and the ORs relating the number of resources to continuation will be the same regardless of marital status.

As shown in Figure 2.21, visually the slope of the regression lines is steeper for one-parent families, implying that the effect of resources is stronger for these families. However, this interaction is not statistically significant and so normally you would not construct and interpret these figures; we are merely doing this for illustrative purposes.

Figures 2.22 and 2.23 indicate essentially the same relationship as Figure 2.21, but odds and probabilities are more easily interpreted and understood. For example, for one-parent families, the odds of continuing increase by a factor of 2.38 in going from two resources below the mean to two above (i.e., OR = 2.38 = 1.50/0.63); for two-parent families, the odds only increase by a factor of 1.26 (i.e., OR = 1.26 = 1.75/1.39). The corresponding probability of continuing, as shown in Figure 2.23, goes from .39 to .60 (an increase of .21) for one-parent families, and from .58 to .64 (an increase of .06) for two-parent families.

In addition to the graphs, sometimes it may also be useful to report the results of interactions in tables. The data tables associated with the above figures illustrate one way this could be done.

Sample Size

When trying to determine sample size for logistic regression, you must be concerned about the number of events in the smaller of the two categories of your DV, in addition to total sample size. Some sources advise at least 10 events for each IV (Peduzzi, Concato, Kemper, Holford, & Feinstein, 1996), although more recent research suggests that 5–9 events may be sufficient under some circumstances, and 10–16 events may be insufficient under other circumstances (Vittinghoff & McCulloch, 2006). Statistical power and the precision of parameter estimates should also be considered carefully in determining sample size. Dattalo (2008) provides a good practical discussion of these issues for logistic regression and a wide range of other statistical methods, including a discussion of available software.

Overview of the Process

Finally, we conclude with an enumeration of the steps involved in a binary logistic regression analysis, and more generally in all of the regression models discussed in this book:

- Select IVs and decide whether to test curvilinear relationships or interactions.
- Carefully screen and clean data, as needed.
- Transform and code variables, as needed.
- Estimate regression model.
- Examine assumptions necessary to estimate binary regression model, examine model fit, and revise the model as needed.

- Test hypotheses about the overall model and specific model parameters, such as ORs.
- Create tables and graphs to present results in the most meaningful and parsimonious way.
- Interpret results of the estimated model in terms of logits, probabilities, odds, and odds ratios, as appropriate.

Additional Regression Models for Dichotomous Dependent Variables

We started this chapter by noting that binary logistic regression is one possible method for analyzing the effects of multiple IVs on a dichotomous DV, and a versatile and widely used one at that. Binary probit regression is a related method that can be used in much the same circumstances as binary logistic regression (Hardin & Hilbe, 2007; Hosmer & Lemeshow, 2000). The choice between these two models is largely one of convenience and discipline-specific convention, because the substantive results are generally indistinguishable. Many researchers prefer binary logistic regression because it provides odds ratios whereas probit regression does not, and binary logistic regression comes with a wider variety of fit statistics.

Complementary log-log (clog-log) and log-log models are alternatives to binary logistic and probit models that may be useful when the probability of the event is very small or very large (Hardin & Hilbe, 2007). Discriminant analysis is an alternative to binary logistic regression, but it has much more restrictive assumptions (Stevens, 2001). Loglinear analysis is another alternative when all of the variables are categorical (Agresti, 2007).

Additional Readings and Web Links

We can recommend a number of good books and chapters in books that cover binary logistic regression in some detail. Chapters on binary logistic regression in Cohen et al. (2003), DeMaris (2004), Fox (2008), Hoffmann (2004), Long and Freese (2006), and Norusis (2006) are useful places to start. Books by Hosmer and Lemeshow (2000), Jaccard (2001), and Pampel (2000) are especially useful.

Numerous published articles provide good examples of the application of binary logistic regression, indeed far too many to list here. For example, Rishel, Greeno, Marcus, Shear, and Anderson (2005) used logistic regression to test the predictive ability of a widely used psychiatric screening tool for children in a community mental health setting. Seven logistic regression models were computed, using CBCL subscale scores as IVs in each model, and seven diagnoses (present or not) derived from structured interviews as the DVs. Litwin and Zoabi (2004) also used logistic regression to predict whether elderly Arab Israelis were abused or not (DV), based on socio-demographic, dependency, modernization, and social integration (IV) variables.

You might find the following Web sites useful resources for binary logistic regression:

http://www2.chass.ncsu.edu/garson/PA765/logistic.htm
http://www.ats.ucla.edu/STAT/spss/topics/logistic_regression.htm
http://www.statisticssolutions.com/Logistic_Regression.htm
http://www.leeds.ac.uk/iss/documentation/tut/tut116/tut116-5.html

SPSS Instructions

Cross-Tabulation

- Start SPSS 16 and open the Chapter 2 data set.
- From the menus choose:
  Analyze
  Descriptive Statistics
  Crosstabs...
- Select the DV (e.g., *Continue Fostering*) and click the arrow button to move it to *Row(s)*.
- Select the IV (e.g., *Married*) and click the arrow button to move it to *Column(s)*.
- Click *Statistics* and then click *Chi-square*. Click *Continue*.
- Click *Cells* and then click *Column*. Click *Continue*.
- Click *OK* to get the results.

z-scores

- Start SPSS 16 and open the Chapter 2 data set.
- From the menus choose:
  Analyze

Descriptive Statistics
Descriptives . . .

- Select the variable to be transformed (e.g., *Resources*) and click the arrow button to move it to *Variable(s)*.
- Click *Save standardized values as variables* to save new variables as *z*-scores.
- Click *OK* to get the results.

Note: After you run the analysis save the data set, which now contains new transformed variable(s).

Binary Logistic Regression (GZLM)

There are two ways to estimate binary logistic regression with SPSS. Let's start with SPSS *GZLM*, and then we'll turn to instructions for binary logistic regression with SPSS *Regression*. However, the only substantive difference is that SPSS *Regression* lets you enter IVs sequentially.

- Start SPSS 16 and open the Chapter 2 data set.
- From the menus choose:

   Analyze
   Generalized Linear Models
   (GZLM) Generalized Linear Models . . .

Generalized Linear Model Dialog Boxes

SPSS *GZLM* contains nine dialog boxes (*Type of Model, Response, Predictors*, etc.). When you first open GZLM you'll see the *Type of Model* dialog box illustrated in Figure 2.24. To select another dialog box, click the associated tab. When you are finished, click *OK* to get the results. Click *Help* to get a more detailed description of options for a particular dialog box. (Note: the bold flush-left headings below correspond to the nine tabs across the top of the dialog box.)

Type of Model

- Click *Binary Logistic*.

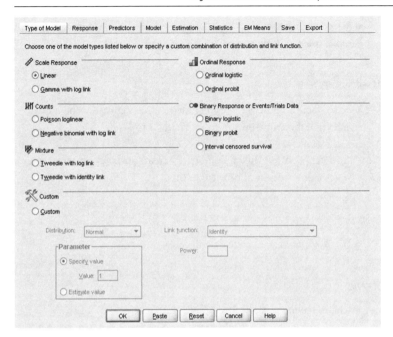

Figure 2.24 Generalized Linear Model Dialog Box: Type of Model

Response

- Select a dichotomous DV (e.g., *ContinueFostering*) and click the arrow button to move it to *Dependent Variable*.

Note: The default reference category for the DV is the last (highest) value of the DV (e.g., 1). Typically you'll want to change this to the first (lowest) value (e.g., 0). To do this, click *Reference Category* and click *First (lowest value)*.

Predictors

- Select categorical IVs (e.g., *Married*, *County*) and click the arrow button to move them to *Factors*.

  - For a polytomous variable, click *Options* and click *Ascending* or *Descending* to use the last or first category, respectively, as the reference category for dummy coding. For a dichotomous variable coded as 0 and 1 typically, *Descending* should be used.

- Select quantitative IVs (e.g., *Resources*) and click the arrow button to move them to *Covariates*.

Model

- Select factors and covariates included as main effects in the model and click the arrow button to move them to *Model*.

Note: You can also use this dialog box to create interaction terms. Click *Help* to get a description of how to do this.

Estimation

- You don't need to change default settings.

Statistics

- Click *Likelihood ratio*, listed under *Chi-square Statistics*.
- Click *Include exponential parameter estimates*, listed under *Print*.

Estimated Marginal (EM) Means

- You don't need to change default settings.

Save

- Click *Predicted value of mean response* to save predicted probabilities.
- Click *Predicted value of linear predictor* to save predicted logits.
- Click *Cook's distance* to save Cook's distance.
- Click *Leverage value* to save leverage values.
- Click *Deviance residual* to save deviance residuals.
- Click *Standardized deviance residual* to save standardized deviance residuals.

Note: After you run the analysis, save the data set, which now contains new variables that you can use to create index plots and for other purposes.

Note: SPSS does not have an option to compute odds for each case. However, odds $= p/1 - p$. So, after using SPSS to compute and save estimated probabilities for each case (i.e., *Predicted value of mean response*), you can use SPSS to compute the odds for each case. For example, if the variable name for probabilities is *MeanPredicted,* you could use the following syntax to compute the odds for each case:

compute odds $=$ *MeanPredicted*/(1 $-$ *MeanPredicted*).

Binary Logistic Regression (Regression)

- Start SPSS 16 and open the Chapter 2 data set.
- From the menus choose:
  Analyze
  Regression
  Binary Logistic . . .
- Select a dichotomous DV (e.g., *ContinueFostering*), and click the arrow button to move it to *Dependent.*
- Select categorical and quantitative IVs (e.g., *zResources, Married*), and click the arrow button to move them to *Covariates.*

  - Click *Next* to enter IVs sequentially, if desired.

- Click *Categorical* and then select categorical IVs and click the arrow button to move them to *Categorical Covariates.*

  - Click Indicator and select the type of coding for each categorical IV (First click *Help* to get a description of possible contrasts.).
  - Click either *First* or *Last* for the reference category, if appropriate.
  - Click *Change*, and then *Continue.*

- Click *Save* and then click *Probabilities, Cook's, Leverage values, Studentized*, and *Deviance.* Click *Continue.*
- Click *Options* and then click *CI for* exp(*B*). Click *Continue.*
- Click *OK* to get the results.

Note: After you run the analysis save the data set, which now contains new variables that you can use to create index plots and for other purposes.

Excel Workbooks

The names of the following seven workbooks correspond to the variables used in the associated binary logistic regression analyses. These workbooks show how we created the figures reported in this chapter for the associated analyses, as well as additional related figures not included.

- Married.xls
- Resources.xls
- zResources.xls
- cResources.xls
- Married & zResources.xls
- cResources & cResources2.xls
- Married, cResources, & MarriedXcResources.xls

This workbook shows how we created the data for Table 2.8.

- p odds logit.xls

This workbook shows how we created the data and graphs for Figures 2.9, 2.10, and 2.11.

- x logit odds p.xls

This workbook lets you compute the difference between two likelihood ratio χ^2 values in order to compare full and reduced models. Enter your data into the highlighted cells and the difference between the two likelihood ratio χ^2 values, the difference between the degrees of freedom, and the associated p value will be computed automatically.

- Chi-square Difference.xls

3

Regression with a Polytomous Dependent Variable

Your investigation of interventions with mothers leaving public welfare is designed to enhance their ability to remain off the welfare rolls. What is your dependent variable? Some similar studies have used a dichotomous variable indicating return to welfare or not, but you realize that this variable would not capture the success of your intervention, so you construct a DV that indicates the reason for leaving welfare: *marriage, stable employment, a move to another state, incarceration*, or *death*.

Polytomous variables such as the outcome variable in the above scenario have three or more unordered categories. Often, these variables are called *multicategorical* or *multinomial* (the assumed underlying distribution). Dichotomous DVs probably are more common, but social workers and those in related areas frequently conduct research in which the DV is polytomous. For example, we have investigated whether foster home applicants are subsequently licensed to foster, discontinue the application process prior to licensure, or are rejected for licensure (Rhodes et al., 2003a). Choi (2003) looked at predictors of changes in living arrangements of the elderly: newly coresiding with their children, no longer coresiding, or residing in institutions.

This chapter describes the use of **multinomial logistic regression** (also known as *polytomous* or *nominal logistic* or *logit regression* or the *discrete choice model*), a versatile and popular method for modeling relationships between a polytomous DV and multiple IVs (Borooah, 2001; DeMaris, 2004; Hoffmann, 2004; Hosmer & Lemeshow, 2000; Long, 1997; Norusis, 2007). Multinomial logistic regression is a generalization of binary logistic regression to a polytomous DV, and when it is applied to a dichotomous DV it is identical to binary logistic regression (Hardin & Hilbe, 2007; Long 1997). So, the basic issues involved in examining the effect of IVs on polytomous DVs are the same as those we discussed in Chapter 2.

Chapter Example

In this chapter, we will discuss and illustrate multinomial logistic regression by examining variables that influence the effort needed to interview and track 246 mothers of newborns over time (Combs-Orme, Cain, & Wilson, 2004; Wilson, 2006). The DV, interview tracking effort (variable name *TrackCat*), consists of three mutually exclusive and exhaustive categories of mothers: (1) 149 (60.60%) easy-to-interview-and-track mothers (*Easy*); (2) 54 (22.00%) difficult-to-track mothers who required more telephone calls (*MoreCalls*); and (3) 43 (17.48%) difficult-to-track mothers who required more unscheduled home visits (*More Visits*).

We will analyze the effects of maternal race (variable name *Race*) and number of years of education (variable name *Education*) on interview tracking effort. Race is a dichotomous variable, with European American mothers coded as 0 and African American mothers coded as 1. The sample contains 143 (58.1%) European Americans and 103 (41.9%) African Americans. Number of years of education has a fairly normal distribution, with $M = 12.29$ ($SD = 2.14$) and a range from 8 through 17.

Cross-Tabulation and Chi-Squared Test

We start by examining a simple research question: *What is the relationship between race and interview tracking effort?* A cross-tabulation table and chi-squared test let us answer this question and provide a good starting point for understanding multinomial logistic regression. The relationship between *Race* and *TrackCat* is statistically significant $[\chi^2(2, N = 246) = 8.69, p = .013]$. Probabilities, odds, and ORs can help us understand our results more fully, but first we need to decide on a reference category.

In binary logistic regression, the category of the DV coded 0 implicitly serves as the reference category. In multinomial logistic regression, we need to select a reference category explicitly. We'll use *Easy* as the reference category because we were interested in factors that make it more difficult to track. So, we'll compare *More Calls* and *More Visits* to *Easy* when we compute probabilities, odds, and ORs.

We start with the probability of *More Calls*. As you can see in Table 3.1, 30 European Americans required *More Calls* and 96 were *Easy*, so the probability of *More Calls* equals .24 [30/(30+96)]. In contrast, 24 African Americans required *More Calls* and 53 were *Easy*, so the probability of *More Calls* equals .31 [24/(24+53)]. Notice that the probability of *More Calls* is somewhat higher for African Americans.

We now turn to the probability of *More Visits*. As you can see in Table 3.1, 17 European Americans required *More Visits* and 96 were *Easy*, so the probability of *More Visits* equals .15 [17/(17 + 96)]. In contrast, 26 African Americans required *More Visits* and 53 were *Easy*, so the probability of *More Visits* equals .33 [26/(26 + 53)]. The probability of *More Visits* is considerably higher for African Americans.

Table 3.1 Interview Tracking Status as a Function of Race

| | | | Race | | |
			European American	African American	Total
Interview Tracking Effort Categories	(1) Easy	Count % within Race	96 67.13	53 51.46	149 60.57
	(2) More Calls	Count % within Race	30 20.98	24 23.30	54 21.95
	(3) More Visits	Count % within Race	17 11.9	26 25.24	43 17.48
Total		Count % within Race	143 100.00	103 100.00	246 100.00

Now, let us calculate odds and ORs from the cross-tabulation. The odds that mothers require *More Calls*, compared to *Easy*, are .3125 (i.e., 0.2098/0.6713) for European Americans and .4528 (i.e., 0.2330/0.5146) for African Americans. The OR equals 1.45 (i.e., .4528 /.3125), indicating that the odds of requiring *More Calls*, compared to being *Easy*, are higher for African Americans by a factor of 1.45. You could also say that being African American increases the odds of requiring more calls, compared to being easy-to-track, by 45% [100(1.45 − 1)] 1.45 − 1.

The odds that mothers require more visits, compared to *Easy*, are .1771 (i.e., 0.1189/0.6713) for European Americans and .4905 (i.e., 0.2524/0.5146) for African Americans. The OR equals 2.77 (i.e., .4905/ .1771), indicating that the odds of requiring more visits, compared to being easy-to-track, are higher for African Americans by a factor of 2.77. You could also say that being African American increases the odds of requiring more visits, compared to being easy-to-track, by 177% [100(2.77 − 1)].

One Dichotomous Independent Variable

Multinomial logistic regression is identical to binary logistic regression when the DV has only two values. Indeed, binary logistic regression can be seen as a special case of the multinomial logistic model in which the DV has only two categories (Hardin & Hilbe, 2007; Long, 1997).

Multinomial logistic regression can be thought of as a set of binary logistic regression models that are estimated simultaneously. Just as with binary logistic regression, one value of the DV is designated as the reference category, and we selected *Easy*. In binary and multinomial logistic regression, each category of the DV is compared to the reference category. However, multinomial logistic regression involves two or more such comparisons, and a separate equation is estimated for each comparison. This makes it a bit more difficult to interpret multinomial logistic regression results, but it follows the same basic ideas we discussed in Chapter 2 for binary logistic regression.

In our example, two binary regression models are estimated simultaneously and, as in Chapter 2, L symbolizes the estimated logit. With multinomial logistic regression, the number of binary models estimated is one fewer than the number of categories of the DV. (Again, this is just like binary logistic regression where the DV has two categories and one model is estimated.)

Tables 3.2, 3.3, and 3.4 show partial results of the multinomial logistic regression. From Table 3.4, the estimated multinomial logistic regression equations are:

$$L_{(\text{More Calls vs. Easy})} = -1.163 + (.371)(X_{\text{Race}})$$

$$L_{(\text{More Visits vs. Easy})} = -1.731 + (1.019)(X_{\text{Race}})$$

As shown in Table 3.2, the relationship between *Race* and *Track-Cat* is statistically significant. This likelihood ratio chi-squared test provides a test of the overall null hypothesis that all slopes equal 0 ($\beta_{(\text{Race, More Calls vs. Easy})} = \beta_{(\text{Race, More Visits vs. Easy})} = 0$). Table 3.3 provides a likelihood ratio χ^2 *test* that each of the two slopes for race equals 0 ($\beta_{(\text{Race, More Calls vs. Easy})} = \beta_{(\text{Race, More Visits vs. Easy})} = 0$). With a single IV, these two likelihood ratio χ^2 tests are identical.

Table 3.4 provides a Wald test for each slope. We see no statistically significant relationship between *Race* and *More Calls* compared to *Easy*, but we do identify a statistically significant relationship between *More Visits* and *Easy*. The OR for this latter comparison is 2.77, indicating that the odds of *More Visits*, compared to *Easy*, are higher for African Americans by a factor of 2.77. You could also say that being

Table 3.2 Model Fitting Information

Model	Model Fitting Criteria	Likelihood Ratio Tests		
	−2 Log Likelihood	Chi-Square	df	Sig.
Intercept Only	27.610			
Final	18.990	8.620	2	.013

Table 3.3 Likelihood Ratio Tests

Effect	Model Fitting Criteria	Likelihood Ratio Tests		
	−2 Log Likelihood of Reduced Model	Chi-Square	df	Sig.
Intercept	90.575	71.585	2	.000
Race	27.610	8.620	2	.013

Table 3.4 Parameter Estimates

Interview Tracking Effort Categories[a]		B	Std. Error	Wald	df	Sig.	Exp(B)	95% CI Exp(B)	
								Lower Bound	Upper Bound
(2) More Calls	Intercept	−1.163	.209	30.924	1	.000			
	Race	.371	.323	1.319	1	.251	1.449	.769	2.729
(3) More Visits	Intercept	−1.731	.263	43.282	1	.000			
	Race	1.019	.356	8.203	1	.004	2.770	1.379	5.564

[a] The reference category is: (1) Easy.

African American increases the odds of requiring more visits, compared to being easy-to-track, by 177% [100(2.77 − 1)]. (This is the same OR we calculated above from the cross-tabulation.) Finally, note that as in binary logistic regression, ORs are exponentiated values of the slopes (i.e., $e^{.371} = 1.45$ and $e^{1.019} = 2.77$).

Estimated values of logits, odds, and probabilities can be calculated using the estimated multinomial regression equations in the same way as for binary logistic models, as described in Chapter 2. For example, estimated logits for African Americans ($X = 1$) are:

$$L_{(\text{More Calls vs. Easy})} = -.792 = -1.163 + (.371)\,(1)$$
$$L_{(\text{More Visits vs. Easy})} = -.712 = -1.731 + (1.019)\,(1)$$

Figure 3.1 illustrates the estimated logits. Logits for *More Calls* and *More Visits* are higher for African Americans (although the former relationship is not statistically significant).

Estimated odds are obtained by exponentiating the logits. For example, estimated odds for African Americans are:

$$Odds_{(\text{More Calls vs. Easy})} = e^{-.792} = .45$$
$$Odds_{(\text{More Visits vs. Easy})} = e^{-.712} = .49$$

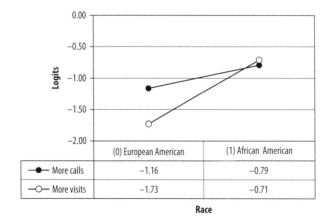

Figure 3.1 Effect of Race on Interview Tracking Effort (Logits)

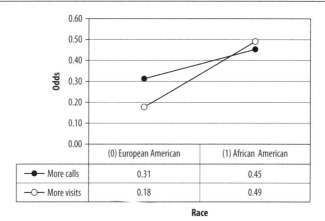

Figure 3.2 Effect of Race on Interview Tracking Effort (Odds)

See Figure 3.2 for the estimated odds. The odds of *More Calls* and *More Visits* are higher for African Americans (although the former relationship is not statistically significant). Compare the odds shown in Figure 3.2 to those computed using the cross-tabulation and note that they are exactly the same.

Estimated probabilities are obtained using the inverse link function. For example, estimated probabilities for African Americans are:

$$\hat{p}_{\text{(More Calls vs. Easy)}} = \frac{e^{-.792}}{1 + e^{-.792}} = .31$$

$$\hat{p}_{\text{(More Visits vs. Easy)}} = \frac{e^{-.712}}{1 + e^{-.712}} = .33$$

Figure 3.3 shows the estimated probabilities. The probabilities of *More Calls* and *More Visits* are lower for European Americans (although the former relationship is not statistically significant). Compare the probabilities in Figure 3.3 to those computed using the cross-tabulation and note that they are exactly the same.

Reference Category

In binary and multinomial logistic regression, the reference category (sometimes called a *baseline, base, or comparison* category) usually is the absence of an event or characteristic, although this is not necessary and

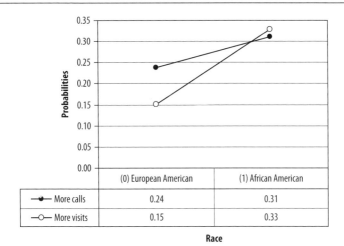

Figure 3.3 Effect of Race on Interview Tracking Effort (Probabilities)

it depends on the research question. In Chapter 2, we used *discontinue fostering* as the reference category because we formulated the research question in terms of variables that influence families to *continue fostering*. However, we could just as easily have formulated our research question in terms of variables that influence families to discontinue fostering. In our current example, we used easy-to-track as the reference category because we were interested in factors that make it more difficult to track.

Your choice of a reference group affects your results. For example, suppose we use *More Visits* as the reference group; our resulting comparisons would be *Easy* compared to *More Visits* and *More Calls* compared to *More Visits*. Table 3.5 shows partial regression results with *More Visits* as the reference category.

When we used *Easy* as the reference group, we did not compare *More Calls* to *More Visits*, so the comparison of *More Calls* to *More Visits* is an entirely new comparison. Also, when we used *Easy* as the reference group we compared *More Visits* to *Easy*, but when we used *More Visits* as the reference group we compared *Easy* to *More Visits*. So, as you will notice in Table 3.5, the sign of the slope for *Easy* compared to *More Visits* (-1.019) is reversed, and the OR is the reciprocal ($1/2.77 = 0.361$).

What should you do if you have an interest in all possible comparisons (e.g., *More Calls* and *Easy, More Visits* and *Easy,* and *More Calls*

Table 3.5 Parameter Estimates

Interview Tracking Effort Categories[a]		B	Std. Error	Wald	df	Sig.	Exp(B)	95% CI Exp(B)	
								Lower Bound	Upper Bound
(1) Easy	Intercept	1.731	.263	43.282	1	.000			
	Race	−1.019	.356	8.203	1	.004	.361	.180	0.725
(2) More Calls	Intercept	.568	.304	3.501	1	.061			
	Race	−.648	.415	2.437	1	.118	.523	.232	1.180

[a] The reference category is: (3) More Visits.

and *More Visits*), such as might be the case if no natural reference category exists? Simply run the multinomial logistic regression twice, each time with a different reference category, as we did above.

The number of comparisons possible in a multinomial logistic regression is $m(m-1)/2$, where m is the number of categories in the DV, so for our three-category variable we can conduct three possible comparisons. However, there are only $m-1$ nonredundant comparisons (DeMaris, 2004). For example, as we saw above when we used *More Visits* as the reference category, *Easy* was again compared to *More Visits*, as it was when we used *Easy* as the reference category, although the direction of the slope and OR was reversed.

One Quantitative Independent Variable

The use and interpretation of multinomial logistic regression are much the same with quantitative and categorical IVs. We will start with a simple example of a single quantitative IV, using number of years of education as the IV. The research question is this: *What is the relationship between number of years of education and tracking effort?*

See Tables 3.6 and 3.7 for partial results of this analysis. As Table 3.6 shows, the overall relationship between education and *TrackCat* is statistically significant. However, as shown in Table 3.7, education has a statistically significant relationship with *More Visits* compared to *Easy*, but not with *More Calls* compared to *Easy*. More specifically, we see a negative relationship between education and *More Visits* versus *Easy* (OR = 0.76). That is, for every additional year of education the odds of needing more visits, compared to being easy-to-track, decrease by a factor of .76. Alternatively, you could say the odds decrease by $24.1\%[100(0.759-1)]$.

Table 3.6 Likelihood Ratio Tests

	Model Fitting Criteria	Likelihood Ratio Tests		
Effect	-2 *Log Likelihood of Reduced Model*	*Chi-Square*	*df*	*Sig.*
Intercept	77.974	3.675	2	.159
Education	85.083	10.784	2	0.005

Table 3.7 Parameter Estimates

Interview Tracking Effort Categories[a]		B	Std. Error	Wald	df	Sig.	Exp(B)	95% CI Exp(B)	
								Lower Bound	Upper Bound
(2) More Calls	Intercept	.583	0.962	.367	1	.545			
	Education	−.130	0.078	2.774	1	.096	.878	.754	1.023
(3) More Visits	Intercept	2.077	1.113	3.484	1	.062			
	Education	−.276	0.094	8.660	1	.003	.759	.631	0.912

[a] The reference category is: (1) Easy.

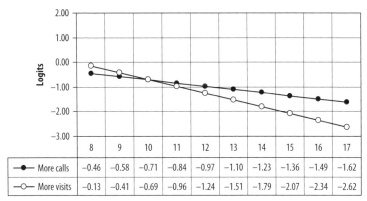

Figure 3.4 Effect of Education on Tracking Effort (Logits)

Estimated logits, odds, and probabilities can be calculated using the estimated multinomial regression equations in the same way as described above for race. For example, estimated logits for mothers with a high school education or equivalent ($X = 12$) are:

$$L_{\text{(More Calls vs. Easy)}} = -0.977 = 0.583 + (-.130)(12)$$
$$L_{\text{(More Visits vs. Easy)}} = -1.235 = 2.077 + (-.276)(12)$$

Figure 3.4 shows the estimated logits. Estimated logits for *More Calls* and *More Visits*, compared to *Easy*, decrease with education.

Estimated odds are obtained by exponentiating the estimated logits. For example, estimated odds for mothers with a high school education or equivalent ($X = 12$) are:

$$Odds_{\text{(More Calls vs. Easy)}} = e^{-.977} = 0.38$$
$$Odds_{\text{(More Visits vs. Easy)}} = e^{-1.235} = 0.29$$

See Figure 3.5 for the estimated odds. You can see that the odds for *More Calls* and *More Visits*, compared to *Easy*, decrease with education. More specifically, for every additional year of education the odds of *More Visits*, compared to *Easy*, decrease by a factor of .76 (i.e., OR = 0.76), or 24.1%. For each additional 4 years of education (e.g., eighth grade to high

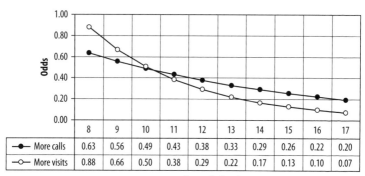

	8	9	10	11	12	13	14	15	16	17
More calls	0.63	0.56	0.49	0.43	0.38	0.33	0.29	0.26	0.22	0.20
More visits	0.88	0.66	0.50	0.38	0.29	0.22	0.17	0.13	0.10	0.07

Years of education

Figure 3.5 Effect of Education on Tracking Effort (Odds)

school, high school to college graduate) the odds decrease by a factor of
.33 (i.e., OR $= 0.33 = e^{(4)(B)} = e^{(4)(-.276)}$), or 67%.

Estimated probabilities are obtained using the inverse link function.
For example, estimated probabilities for mothers with a high school
education or equivalent ($X = 12$) are:

$$\hat{p}_{(\text{More Calls vs. Easy})} = \frac{e^{-.977}}{1 + e^{-.977}} = .27$$

$$\hat{p}_{(\text{More Visits vs. Easy})} = \frac{e^{-1.235}}{1 + e^{-1.235}} = .22$$

Figure 3.6 shows the estimated probabilities. Probabilities for *More Calls*
and *More Visits*, compared to *Easy*, decrease with education. More specifically, the probability of *More Visits* goes from .47 for mothers with an
eighth- grade education, to .22 for mothers with a high school education or equivalent, to .07 for mothers with education beyond 4 years of
college.

Multiple Independent Variables

Here we will build on the previous two examples in this chapter to illustrate multiple multinomial logistic regression. Earlier, we saw that being
African American was associated with the need for more visits, but not
more calls, relative to easy-to-track. We also saw that education was

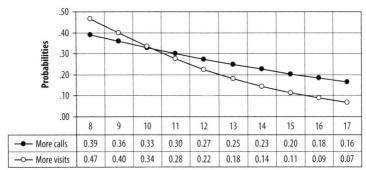

Figure 3.6 Effect of Education on Tracking Effort (Probabilities)

Table 3.8 Model Fitting Information

	Model Fitting Criteria	Likelihood Ratio Tests		
Model	−2 Log Likelihood	Chi-Square	df	Sig.
Intercept Only	139.216			
Final	121.887	17.328	4	.002

Table 3.9 Likelihood Ratio Tests

	Model Fitting Criteria	Likelihood Ratio Tests		
Effect	−2 Log Likelihood of Reduced Model	Chi-Square	df	Sig.
Intercept	123.368	1.480	2	.477
Race	128.432	6.544	2	.038
Education	130.595	8.708	2	.013

associated inversely with more visits, but not more calls, relative to easy-to-track. Oftentimes, race and education are correlated, so the research question examined here is this: *What is the relationship between race and interview tracking effort, when controlling for education?*

See Tables 3.8, 3.9, and 3.10 for partial results of this analysis. The null hypothesis that all four slopes equal 0 can be rejected ($\beta_{(\text{Race, More Calls vs. Easy})} = \beta_{(\text{Race, More Visits vs. Easy})} = \beta_{(\text{Ed, More Calls vs. Easy})} = \beta_{(\text{Ed, More Visits vs. Easy})} = 0$), as shown in Table 3.8. The null hypothesis that the two slopes for race equal 0 can be rejected, and the null hypothesis

Table 3.10 Parameter Estimates

Interview Tracking Effort Categories[a]		B	Std. Error	Wald	df	Sig.	Exp(B)	95% CI Exp(B)	
								Lower Bound	Upper Bound
(2) More Calls	Intercept	.345	.993	.120	1	.729			
	Race	.307	.326	.882	1	.348	1.359	0.717	2.576
	Education	−.120	.078	2.352	1	.125	0.887	0.760	1.034
(3) More Visits	Intercept	1.416	1.176	1.448	1	.229			
	Race	.910	.362	6.330	1	.012	2.485	1.223	5.052
	Education	−.258	.097	7.057	1	.008	0.773	0.639	0.935

[a] The reference category is: (1) Easy.

that the two slopes for education equal 0 can also be rejected, as shown in Table 3.9. That is, race is related to interview tracking effort when controlling for education, and education is related to interview tracking effort when controlling for race.

Race has a statistically significant relationship with *More Visits* compared to *Easy* but not *More Calls* compared to *Easy*, as shown in Table 3.10. More specifically, the odds of more visits are higher for African Americans by a factor of 2.48, when controlling for education (or you could say that the odds are 148% higher). Notice that the OR of 2.48 is not that much different than the OR of 2.77 found above when education was not controlled.

Education has a statistically significant relationship with *More Visits* compared to *Easy* but not *More Calls* compared to *Easy*, as shown in Table 3.10. More specifically, for every additional year of education the odds of more visits decrease by a factor of .77, when controlling for race (or you could say the odds decrease by 23%). Notice that the OR of .77 is virtually identical to the OR of .76 found above when race was not controlled.

From Table 3.10, the multinomial logistic regression equations are:

$$L_{(\text{More Calls vs. Easy})} = .345 + (.307)(X_{\text{Race}}) + (-.120)(X_{\text{Ed}})$$

$$L_{(\text{More Visits vs. Easy})} = 1.416 + (.910)(X_{\text{Race}}) + (-.258)(X_{\text{Ed}})$$

These can be used to compute logits, odds, ORs, and probabilities, as discussed above. To understand and present results of a multinomial logistic regression, you should examine the odds, ORs, and probabilities for substantively informative values (e.g., high school education or equivalent), and for substantively important types of cases (e.g., European Americans and African Americans with a high school education or equivalent). Or, for continuous IVs without inherently informative substantive values, you might compute and report estimated probabilities using the mean and one or two standard deviations above and below the mean (or the 25% and 75% percentiles), fixing all other IVs at selected values (Hoffmann, 2004; Long & Freese, 2006).

Odds for cases with different values of the IVs can be presented in tables. Table 3.11 shows the estimated odds for European Americans and African Americans with three different substantively meaningful levels of education. From this table, you can see, for example, that the odds of

Table 3.11 Estimated Odds as a Function of Education and Race

	Estimated Odds Education		
Race	8th Grade	High School	College
European American			
More Calls	.54	.33	.21
More Visits	.52	.19	.07
African American			
More Calls	.73	.45	.28
More Visits	1.30	.46	.17

needing more visits are better than even for African Americans with an eighth-grade education (odds = 1.30), but low for mothers of any race with a college education.

In addition to presenting odds in tables, it is often useful to present them in figures, such as Figures 3.7 and 3.8, which show the effect of education for European Americans and African Americans, respectively. The larger the number of IVs, though, the more difficult this becomes, and only a limited number of IVs can be represented meaningfully on a single graph. One way to do this is to plot the relationship of one IV from its minimum to maximum value, while all other variables are fixed at their means (or at *0* or *1* for dichotomous IVs). Another strategy is to estimate the odds for selected sets of values of IVs that correspond to

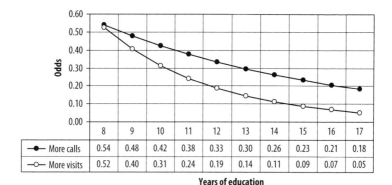

Figure 3.7 Effect of Education on Tracking Effort for European-Americans (Odds)

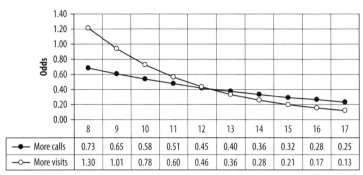

Years of education	8	9	10	11	12	13	14	15	16	17
—●— More calls	0.73	0.65	0.58	0.51	0.45	0.40	0.36	0.32	0.28	0.25
—○— More visits	1.30	1.01	0.78	0.60	0.46	0.36	0.28	0.21	0.17	0.13

Figure 3.8 Effect of Education on Tracking Effort for African-Americans (Odds)

ideal or typical types in the population (e.g., African Americans with a high school education or equivalent) (Long, 1997).

Notice in the above figures that the odds of *More Calls* and *More Visits* decrease with education, but the absolute values of the odds and the pattern of change are different for European Americans and African Americans. Also, note that information from such figures can be used to compute various ORs of importance. For example, for college-educated African Americans, the odds of needing *More Visits* are one-third the odds for European Americans with an eighth-grade education (OR = 0.33 = 0.17/0.52). Or, for college-educated African Americans, the odds of needing *More Visits* are almost the same as the odds for European Americans with a high school education or equivalent (OR = 0.89 = 0.17/0.19).

A good place to begin presenting probabilities is to examine the frequency distributions of the probabilities for all cases, basic descriptive statistics (e.g., mean, median, standard deviation, range, and interquartile range), and different types of univariate charts (histogram, boxplot, etc.). These descriptive statistics are shown in Table 3.12 for our current example. The mean estimated probabilities for *More Calls* and *More Visits* are relatively low, and the variability of these probabilities is relatively low for *More Calls*.

The challenge is to summarize changes in IVs associated with changes in probabilities in the most meaningful and parsimonious way, but no standard way to do this exists. This enterprise is complicated by the fact

Table 3.12 Descriptive Statistics for Estimated Probabilities as a Function of Interview Tracking Status

Statistic	Easy	More Calls	**More Visits**
M	0.61	0.22	0.17
Mdn	0.62	0.23	0.15
SD	0.11	0.03	0.09
Minimum	0.33	0.15	0.04
Maximum	0.81	0.26	0.43
Percentiles			
25	0.52	0.21	0.11
50	0.62	0.23	0.15
75	0.69	0.24	0.24

Table 3.13 Estimated Probabilities as a Function of Education and Race

| | Estimated Probabilities Education | | |
Race	8th Grade	High School	College
European American			
More Calls	.35	.25	.17
More Visits	.34	.16	.06
African American			
More Calls	.42	.31	.22
More Visits	.57	.32	.14

that the relationship between IVs and probabilities is not linear. For any given analysis, you should explore different ways to present the key substantive findings in tables or graphs (Long & Freese, 2006). Again, this depends in part on the subject and objectives of the study.

Probabilities for cases with different values of the IVs can be presented in tables. Table 3.13 shows estimated probabilities for European Americans and African Americans with three different substantively meaningful levels of education. From this table, you can see, for example, that the probability of needing *more visits* ranges from a low of .06 for college-educated European Americans, to a high of .57 for African Americans with an eighth-grade education. You can also see, for example, that the probability of needing *more calls* or *visits* is relatively low for college-educated mothers, regardless of race (i.e., .06 to .22).

In addition to presenting probabilities in tables, it is frequently useful to present them in figures, such as Figures 3.9 and 3.10, which show the

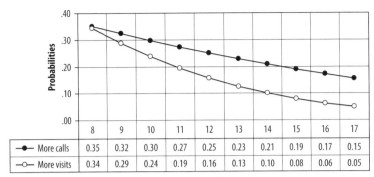

Figure 3.9 Effect of Education on Tracking Effort for European-Americans (Probabilities)

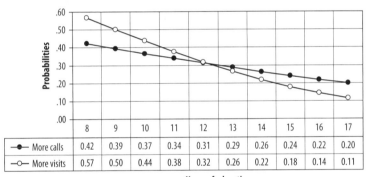

Figure 3.10 Effect of Education on Tracking Effort for African-Americans (Probabilities)

effects of education for European- and African-Americans, respectively. As above, though, this becomes more difficult with more IVs, and a single graph can show a limited number of IVs in a meaningful way. One way to do this is to plot the relationship of one IV from its minimum to maximum value, while all other variables are fixed at their means (or at *0* or *1* for dichotomous IVs). Another strategy is to estimate probabilities for selected sets of values of IVs that correspond to ideal or typical types in the population (e.g., African Americans with college degrees) (Long, 1997).

Notice in the above figures that the probabilities of *More Calls* and *More Visits* decrease with education, but both the absolute values of the probabilities and the pattern of change are different for European Americans and African Americans. For example, for European Americans with an eighth-grade education, the probability of *More Calls* and *More Visits* is about the same (.35 and .34, respectively). For African Americans, both probabilities are higher than for European Americans, and the probability of *More Visits* is higher than *More Calls* (.57 and .42, respectively).

Collapsing Categories of the Dependent Variable

Race and education distinguish between *More Visits* and *Easy* but not between *More Calls* and *Easy*, as we have seen in all of the analyses so far in this chapter. Therefore, in the interest of parsimony, it might be useful to collapse the *More Calls* and *Easy* categories into a single category, which we will label *LessDifficult*, and then create a new variable consisting of two categories: *LessDifficult* (0) and *More Visits* (1) (see DeMaris, 2004, for a discussion of a more formal test of "collapsibility"). We used the following SPSS syntax to create this new dichotomous variable, *TrackCat2*:

recode TrackCat (1 = 0) (2 = 0) (3 = 1) into TrackCat2.

That is, *TrackCat2* equals 0 when *TrackCat* is 1 (*Easy*) or 2 (*More Calls*), and it equals 1 when *TrackCat* is 3 (*More Visits*).

After the new dichotomous DV was constructed, we ran a binary logistic regression analysis using the new dichotomous DV. Table 3.14 shows partial results of this analysis. As you can see, these results are very similar to those shown in Table 3.10 concerning the effect of race and education on *More Visits* as compared to *Easy*.

A Comparison of Multinomial and Binary Logistic Regression

At the beginning of this chapter, we noted that multinomial logistic regression is a generalization of binary logistic regression to a polytomous DV, and when it is applied to a dichotomous DV, it is identical to binary logistic regression. To illustrate this point, we used the

Table 3.14 Parameter Estimates

| Parameter | B | Std. Error | 95% Wald CI | | Hypothesis Test | | | Exp(B) | 95% Wald CI Exp(B) | |
			Lower	Upper	Wald Chi-Square	df	Sig.		Lower	Upper
(Intercept)	.722	1.1354	−1.503	2.948	.405	1	.525	2.059	0.222	19.061
[Race = 1]	.823	.3487	0.139	1.506	5.569	1	.018	2.277	1.150	4.510
Education	−.224	.0940	−.409	−.040	5.700	1	.017	0.799	0.664	0.961

multinomial logistic regression procedure described at the end of this chapter to reanalyze the effect of race and education on the dichotomous interview tracking variable, *TrackCat2*. Table 3.15 shows partial results of this multinomial logistic regression. Compare Tables 3.14 and 3.15 and, as you can see, the results are exactly the same.

We also noted earlier in this chapter that multinomial logistic regression can be thought of as a set of binary logistic regression models that are estimated simultaneously. In binary and multinomial logistic regression, each category of the DV is compared to the reference category, but multinomial logistic regression involves two or more such comparisons, and a separate equation is estimated for each comparison. Let's illustrate this.

First, we used the following SPSS syntax to create two new dichotomous variables, *More Calls* and *More Visits*, by recoding the original DV, *TrackCat* (*Interview Tracking Effort*), into two new variables:

recode TrackCat (1 = 0) (2 = 1) (3 = sysmis) into More Calls.
recode TrackCat (1 = 0) (2 = sysmis) (3 = 1) into More Visits.

More Calls equals 0 when *TrackCat* is 1 (*Easy*), equals 1 when *TrackCat* is 2 (*More Calls*), and missing when *TrackCat* is 3 (*More Visits*). *More Visits* equals 0 when *TrackCat* is 1 (*Easy*), missing when *TrackCat* is 2 (*More Calls*), and equals 1 when *TrackCat* is 3 (*More Visits*).

Next, we ran two separate binary logistic regressions, one with *More Calls* (versus *Easy*) as the DV, and the other with *More Visits* (versus *Easy*) as the DV. Table 3.16 shows partial results of the binary logistic regression for *More Calls*, and Table 3.17 shows partial results of the binary logistic regression for *More Visits*. Compare results in these two tables to results in Table 3.10 in which we used multinomial regression with *Easy* as the reference category. Race has a statistically significant relationship with *More Visits* compared to *Easy* but not *More Calls* compared to *Easy*, as shown in Table 3.10 and in Tables 3.16 and 3.17. Education has a statistically significant relationship with *More Visits* compared to *Easy* but not *More Calls* compared to *Easy*, as shown in Table 3.10 and in Tables 3.16 and 3.17.

Although results shown in Table 3.10 are similar to those shown in Tables 3.16 and 3.17, they are not identical. The basic reason they are not identical is that multinomial logistic regression estimates the entire

Table 3.15 Parameter Estimates

| TrackingCat2[a] | | B | Std. Error | Wald | df | Sig. | Exp(B) | 95% CI Exp(B) | |
								Lower Bound	Upper Bound
More Visits	Intercept	.722	1.135	.405	1	.525			
	Race	.823	.349	5.569	1	.018	2.277	1.150	4.510
	Education	−.224	.094	5.700	1	.017	0.799	0.664	0.961

[a] The reference category is: (0) LessDifficult.

Table 3.16 Parameter Estimates

| Parameter | B | Std. Error | 95% Wald CI | | Hypothesis Test | | | Exp(B) | 95% Wald CI Exp(B) | |
			Lower	Upper	Wald Chi-Square	df	Sig.		Lower	Upper
(Intercept)	.335	.9825	−1.591	2.261	.116	1	.733	1.398	0.204	9.591
[Race = 1]	.315	.3261	−.324	.954	.934	1	.334	1.371	0.723	2.597
Education	−.120	.0778	−.272	.033	2.374	1	.123	0.887	0.762	1.033

Table 3.17 Parameter Estimates

| Parameter | B | Std. Error | 95% Wald CI | | Hypothesis Test | | | Exp(B) | 95% Wald CI Exp(B) | |
			Lower	Upper	Wald Chi-Square	df	Sig.		Lower	Upper
(Intercept)	−1.047	1.1401	−3.281	1.188	.843	1	.359	0.351	0.038	3.280
[Race = 1]	−.882	0.3631	−1.594	−.170	5.900	1	.015	0.414	0.203	0.843
Education	.226	0.0933	.043	.409	5.870	1	.015	1.254	1.044	1.505

model simultaneously using the entire sample. The two binary logistic regressions, on the other hand, are each based on part of the sample. That is, the binary logistic regression using *More Calls* as the DV includes only the *More Calls* and *Easy* groups ($n = 203$), but not the *More Visits* group ($n = 43$); the binary logistic regression using *More Visits* as the DV includes only the *More Visits* and *Easy* groups ($n = 192$), but not the *More Calls* group ($n = 54$). The advantage of multinomial logistic regression, when the DV has three or more categories, is that the entire sample is analyzed simultaneously.

Interactions and Curvilinear Relationships

Interactions and curvilinear relationships can be examined with multinomial logistic regression (Jaccard, 2001). You use the same principles and methods to do this as with binary logistic regression. However, interpretation and presentation of the results are complicated by the fact that you need to consider results from more than one regression equation and, of course, this complexity increases as the number of categories of the DV increases.

Assumptions Necessary for Testing Hypotheses

Other than the assumptions we discussed in Chapter 1 (pp. 21–28), we must deal with only one assumption that is unique to multinomial logistic regression. That is, multinomial logistic regression assumes the *independence of irrelevant alternatives (IIA)* (Hoffmann, 2004; Long & Freese, 2006). This peculiar phrase is also used in decision theory. In that context, for example, IIA means that your choice of Candidate A over Candidate B in the election is not influenced by whether Candidate X joins the fray. In the current context, the assumption is that the odds of one outcome (e.g., *More Calls*) relative to another (e.g., *Easy*) are not influenced by other alternatives (e.g., *More Visits*). That is, the odds of *More Calls* relative to *Easy* will be the same whether or not *More Visits* is an alternative (i.e., *More Visits* is irrelevant), or the odds of *More Visits* relative to *Easy* will be the same whether or not *More Calls* is an alternative (i.e., *More Calls* is irrelevant).

Statistical tests are available to test the IIA, but these are not available with SPSS. Moreover, Cheng and Long (2007) demonstrated that these tests are not practical for applied statistics. They recommend a logical approach to assessing whether the outcomes are distinct and independent.

Methods for detecting outliers and influential observations are not well developed for multinomial logistic regression. However, you can create a set of binary DVs from the polytomous DV, run separate binary logistic regressions, and use binary logistic regression methods to detect outliers and influential observations (Hoffmann, 2004; Hosmer & Lemeshow, 2000). For our example, you could use the following SPSS syntax to create two new dichotomous variables, *More Calls* and *More Visits*, by recoding the original DV, *TrackCat* (*Interview Tracking Effort*), into two new variables:

```
recode TrackCat ( 1 = 0) ( 2 = 1) ( 3 = sysmis) into More Calls.
recode TrackCat ( 1 = 0) ( 2 = sysmis) ( 3 = 1) into More Visits.
```

These are the same two dichotomous variables we discussed when we compared multinomial and binary logistic regression.

After the new dichotomous DVs are constructed, run separate binary logistic regression analyses for each new dichotomous DV. Then, examine index plots for leverage values, standardized or unstandardized deviance residuals, and Cook's D as discussed in Chapter 2. For example, Figure 3.11 shows the index plot of standardized deviance residuals for a binary logistic regression with *Education* and *Race* as the IVs and *More Visits* as the DV. No cases have markedly different values from the other cases, and no residual is less than -2 or much more than $+2$.

Multicollinearity

You examine multicollinearity the same way with multinomial logistic regression as with other regression models discussed in this book. For our example with two IVs, tolerance equals .98 and the variance inflation factor equals 1.02, indicating no concern with multicollinearity.

Additional Regression Models for Polytomous Dependent Variables

We started this chapter by noting that multinomial logistic regression is the method used most frequently for analyzing the effects of multiple IVs on a polytomous DV. Multinomial probit regression is a related method

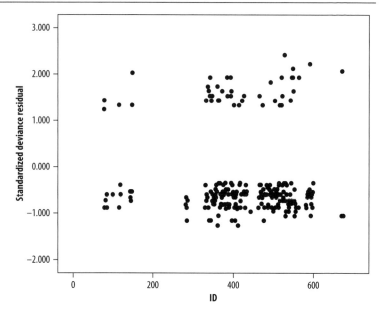

Figure 3.11 Index Plot of Standardized Deviance Residuals

that can be used in much the same circumstances as multinomial logistic regression (Long & Freese, 2006). The choice between these two models is largely one of convenience and discipline-specific convention, because the substantive results are generally indistinguishable. Many researchers prefer multinomial logistic regression, because it provides odds ratios and there is a wider variety of fit statistics available.

Discriminant analysis is also an alternative to multinomial logistic or probit regression, but it has much more restrictive assumptions (Stevens, 2001). Loglinear analysis is another alternative when all of the variables are categorical (Agresti, 2007).

Additional Readings and Web Links

For good chapters discussing multinomial logistic regression, we recommend Borooah (2001), DeMaris (2004); Hoffmann (2004); Hosmer and Lemeshow (2000), Long (1997), and Norusis (2007).

Several published articles provide good examples of the application of multinomial logistic regression. Courtney (1998) used multinomial regression to study factors related to child welfare workers' preferences for different types of foster care settings for children. IVs included characteristics of the child and family, including categorical (e.g., race) and interval-level variables (e.g., age). The DV measured workers' preferences for foster, group, foster family, or kinship care.

In a prospective longitudinal study, Oxford, Gilchrist, Gillmore, and Lohr (2006) used five risk factors (IVs) such as history of school problems and delinquency to predict life course pathways for adolescent mothers. The DV was membership in one of three outcome groups at ages 17 to 23: normative, problem-prone, and psychologically vulnerable.

You might find the following Web sites useful resources for multinomial logistic regression:

http://www2.chass.ncsu.edu/garson/PA765/logistic.htm
http://www.statisticssolutions.com/Logistic_Regression.htm
http://www.education.man.ac.uk/rgsweb/EDUC61022_2006_lec09.pdf
http://www.ats.ucla.edu/stat/Stata/library/odds_ratio_mlogit.htm

SPSS Instructions

Multinomial Logistic Regression (Regression)

Multinomial logistic regression can't be estimated with SPSS *GZLM*. It can be estimated with SPSS *Regression*.

- Start SPSS 16 and open the Chapter 3 data set.
- From the menus choose:
  Analyze
  Regression
  Multinomial Logistic...
- Select a polytomous DV (e.g., *TrackCat*) and click the arrow button to move it to *Dependent*.
- Click *Reference Category* and select the reference category (e.g., *First Category* for *TrackCat* since *Easy* is the first category and it's the reference category.).
- Click "Continue"

- Select polytomous IVs and click the arrow button to move them to *Factor(s)*. (There are no polytomous IVs in this model.)
- Select dichotomous (e.g., *Race*) and quantitative (e.g., *Education*) IVs and click the arrow button to move them to *Covariate(s)*.
- Click *Save* and click *Estimated response probabilities* to save predicted probabilities for each case, for each category of the DV. Click *Continue*.
- Click *OK* to get the results.

Note: In most cases, you won't need to make changes to defaults in the *Model*, *Statistics*, *Criteria*, or *Options* dialog boxes.

Note: After you run the analysis save the data set, which now contains new variables that you can use to create index plots and for other purposes.

Excel Workbooks

The names of the following three workbooks correspond to the variables used in the associated multinomial logistic regression analyses. These workbooks show how we created the figures reported in this chapter for the associated analyses, as well as additional related figures not included.

- Race.xls
- Education.xls
- Race & Education.xls

4

Regression with an Ordinal Dependent Variable

A researcher initiates a new intervention designed to improve the activities of daily living of seniors in congregate living. She measures the outcomes of the intervention by testing the seniors on their competence to perform a number of important tasks, rating each task as 0 (*unable to perform*), 1 (*performs with assistance*), 2 (*performs independently with encouragement*), or 3 (*performs independently without encouragement*).

Ordinal variables such as the one described above have three or more ordered categories. Sometimes these variables are called *ordered categorical variables* or *ordered polytomous variables*. Social workers and those in related areas frequently conduct research in which the DV is ordinal. For example, we have investigated variables associated with the severity of child abuse injury (*none, mild, moderate,* or *severe*) (Zuravin, Orme, & Hegar, 1994), and willingness to foster children with different emotional or behavioral problems (*least acceptable, willing to discuss,* or *most acceptable*) (Cox, Orme, & Rhodes, 2003). Scott (2006) predicted job satisfaction (*very dissatisfied, somewhat dissatisfied, neutral, somewhat satisfied,* or *very satisfied*) among former welfare recipients.

In this chapter, we discuss ordinal logistic regression (also known as the *ordinal logit, ordered polytomous logit, constrained cumulative logit, proportional odds, parallel regression,* or *grouped continuous* model), a versatile and popular method for modeling relationships between an ordinal DV and multiple IVs (Borooah, 2002; Cohen et al., 2003; DeMaris, 2004; Hoffmann, 2004; Hosmer & Lemeshow, 2000; Long, 1997; Long & Freese, 2006; Norusis, 2007). Ordinal logistic regression is a generalization of binary logistic regression to an ordinal DV, and the multinomial distribution is the assumed underlying distribution. When the DV is dichotomous, ordinal logistic regression is identical to binary logistic regression (Long & Freese, 2006). As you will see, the basic issues involved in examining the effect of IVs on an ordinal DV are the same as those discussed in Chapters 2 and 3.

Chapter Example

In this chapter, we will discuss and illustrate ordinal logistic regression by examining variables that influence foster mothers' satisfaction with their foster care agencies. Satisfaction with foster care agencies is the DV (variable name *Satisfaction*). In the sample of 300 foster mothers, 62 (20.7%) rated themselves as *dissatisfied* (1), 68 (22.7%) as *neither satisfied nor dissatisfied* (2), and 170 (56.7%) as *satisfied* (3).

We will analyze the effects of two IVs. One is mothers' reports of whether agencies provided sufficient information about the role of foster care workers (variable name *InfoFCWorker*), a dichotomous variable coded 0 (*no*) and 1 (*yes*). The sample contains 161 (53.7%) mothers who reported they did not receive sufficient information and 139 (46.3%) who reported that they did. We will also examine available time to foster, measured using the Available Time Scale (ATS) (variable name *Time*). The ATS has a potential range of values from 0 through 100, and higher scores indicate more time to foster ($M = 77.16$, $SD = 12.75$).

Cross-Tabulation and Chi-Squared Test

Let us start by examining a simple research question: *Are foster mothers who report that they were provided sufficient information about the role of foster care workers more satisfied with their foster care agencies?* A cross-tabulation table and chi-squared test let us answer this question and also provide a good starting point for understanding ordinal logistic regression.

The relationship between information provided about the role of foster care workers and satisfaction with foster care agencies is statistically significant $[\chi^2(2, N = 300) = 23.52, p < .001]$. However, this just tells us that information and satisfaction are related; it does not give us specific-enough information to answer our research question. Probabilities, odds, and ORs can help us understand our results more fully.

Binary and multinomial logistic regression focus on probabilities for individual categories of the DV (e.g., the probability that an event will occur) and on odds and ORs based on these probabilities. Ordinal logistic regression focuses on cumulative probabilities of the DV and odds and ORs based on cumulative probabilities. By **cumulative probability** we mean the probability that the DV is less than or equal to a particular value (e.g., 1, 2, or 3 in our example). This takes account of the fact that the DV is ordinal.

As you can see in Table 4.1, for mothers who received insufficient information, the cumulative probability of being dissatisfied is .2857, dissatisfied or neutral .5590 (.2857 + .2733), and dissatisfied, neutral, or satisfied 1.00 (.2867 + .2733 + .4410). For mothers who received sufficient information, the cumulative probability of being dissatisfied is .1151, dissatisfied or neutral .2878 (.1151 + .1727), and dissatisfied, neutral, or satisfied 1.00 (.1151 + .1727 + .7121). These cumulative probabilities are plotted in Figure 4.1 (except for the total cumulative probabilities for the highest value of the DV because they will always sum to 1). As expected, the probability of being dissatisfied, as well as the probability of being either dissatisfied or neutral, is greater for mothers who received insufficient information.

Another feature of ordinal logistic regression is that probabilities, odds, and ORs for values of the DV lower than or equal to a particular value are compared to (i.e., divided by) those for higher values of the DV. This is the reverse of what you do in binary and multinomial logistic regression. This makes it a little more difficult to interpret the probabilities, odds, and ORs from ordinal logistic regression, especially after you have become accustomed to interpreting results from binary and multinomial logistic regression.

With ordinal logistic regression, you calculate odds using cumulative probabilities, and sometimes these odds are called *cumulative odds*. The probability that the DV is less than or equal to a particular value is compared to the probability that it is greater than that value. In our

Table 4.1 Satisfaction with Foster Care Agencies as a Function of Information About the Role of the Foster Care Worker

| | | | Information About Role of Foster Care Worker | | |
			(0) Insufficient	(1) Sufficient	Total
Satisfaction	Dissatisfied	Count	46	16	62
		% within Information about Role of Foster Care Worker	28.57	11.51	20.67
	Neither	Count	44	24	68
		% within Information about Role of Foster Care Worker	27.33	17.27	22.67
	Satisfied	Count	71	99	170
		% within Information about Role of Foster Care Worker	44.10	71.22	56.67
	Total	Count	161	139	300
		% within Information about Role of Foster Care Worker	100.00	100.00	100.00

example, the probability that the DV is 1 (*dissatisfied*) would be compared to the probability that it is either 2 or 3 (*neutral* or *satisfied*); the probability that the DV is 1 or 2 (*dissatisfied* or *neutral*) would be compared to the probability that it is 3 (*satisfied*); and these probabilities would be calculated separately for mothers who did and did not receive sufficient information. (The probability that the DV is 1, 2, or 3 must be 1.00 because there are only three categories, so the last category does not have any associated odds.)

For mothers who received insufficient information, the odds of being dissatisfied (compared to neutral or satisfied) equal .4000 [.2857/ (1 − .2857)], and for mothers who received sufficient information, the

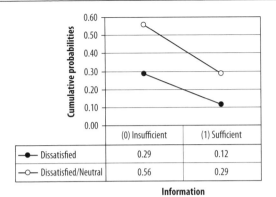

Figure 4.1 Effect of Information on Satisfaction
(Cumulative Probabilities)

odds are .1301 [.1151/(1 − .1151)]. For mothers who received insufficient information, the odds of being dissatisfied or neutral (compared to satisfied) are 1.2676 [.5590/(1 − .5590)], and for mothers who received sufficient information they are .4041 [.2878/(1 − .2878)]. As expected, the odds of being dissatisfied, and the odds of being dissatisfied or neutral, are higher for mothers who received insufficient information.

We use cumulative odds to calculate ORs. The OR that mothers who received sufficient information (compared to mothers who did not) are dissatisfied (compared to neutral or satisfied) equals .33 (.1301/.4000). The OR that mothers who received sufficient information (compared to those who did not) are dissatisfied or neutral (compared to satisfied) equals .32 (.4041/1.2676). These ORs can be expressed in different ways. For the OR of .32, for example, you might say:

The odds of being dissatisfied or neutral (compared to being satisfied) are .32 times smaller for mothers who received sufficient information.

The odds of being dissatisfied or neutral (compared to being satisfied) are 68% lower for mothers who received sufficient information [100(.32 − 1)].

Or, given that ORs greater than 1 are easier for most people to understand, you might compute the reciprocal of the OR and say:

The odds of being dissatisfied or neutral (compared to being satisfied) are 3.13 (1/.32) times larger for mothers who received insufficient information.

The odds of being dissatisfied or neutral (compared to satisfied) are 213%
higher for mothers who received insufficient information [100(3.13 − 1)].

In summary, the OR for dissatisfied (compared to neutral or satisfied) equals .33. The OR for dissatisfied or neutral (compared to
satisfied) equals .32. As we will see next, though, ordinal logistic regression assumes that these ORs are equal in the population (although they
might be different in a sample due to sampling error), and only a single
common OR is estimated. This is called the *proportional odds* or *parallel*
regression assumption, and we discuss it more below.

One Dichotomous Independent Variable

Ordinal logistic regression is identical to binary logistic regression when
the DV has only two values. Indeed, binary logistic regression can be seen
as a special case of the ordinal regression model in which the ordinal DV
has only two categories (e.g., not satisfied or satisfied) (Long & Freese,
2006).

We can think of ordinal logistic regression as a set of binary logistic
regression models that are estimated simultaneously. As with multinomial logistic regression, the number of nonredundant binary logistic
regression equations equals the number of categories of the DV minus
one. Unlike multinomial logistic regression, the focus with ordinal logistic regression is on cumulative probabilities and odds, and ORs are
computed from cumulative odds.

Another feature of ordinal logistic regression that we mentioned
above, but that bears repeating, is that probabilities, odds, and ORs for
values of the DV lower than or equal to a particular value are compared
to (i.e., divided by) those for higher values of the DV. This is the reverse
of what is done in binary and multinomial logistic regression.

Finally, the concept of a *threshold*, sometimes called a *cut-point*, is
necessary for understanding ordinal logistic regression. You can think
of a threshold this way: Suppose our three-point ordinal satisfaction
measure is a rough measure of an underlying continuous satisfaction
variable. At a certain point on this continuous variable, the population
threshold (symbolized by τ, the Greek letter *tau*), that is, a person's level
of satisfaction, goes from one value to another on the ordinal measure

of satisfaction. In our example then, the first threshold (τ_1) would be the point at which the level of satisfaction goes from dissatisfied to neutral (i.e., 1–2), and the second threshold (τ_2) would be the point at which the level of satisfaction goes from neutral to satisfied (i.e., 2–3). The number of thresholds is always one fewer than the number of values of the DV.

Thresholds can range from negative to positive infinity, and the scale on which they are measured has no intrinsic meaning because the scale on which the underlying continuous variable is based is arbitrary. (Similarly, actual values of an ordinal DV are irrelevant except insofar as larger values are considered higher in some sense.) Also, thresholds are not necessarily equally spaced, given that the variable is ordinal. Usually thresholds are of little interest except in the calculation of estimated values. That is, thresholds typically are used in place of the intercept to express the ordinal logistic regression model (Hardin & Hilbe, 2007). (This is the case with SPSS, but not with all software [Long, 1997; Long & Freese, 2006]).

In our example, two binary regression models are estimated simultaneously, where t_1 and t_2 are the estimated thresholds:

$$L_{(\text{Dissatisfied vs. Neutral/Satisfied})} = t_1 - B_{\text{InfoFCWorker}}X_{\text{InfoFCWorker}}$$

$$L_{(\text{Dissatisfied/Neutral vs. Satisfied})} = t_2 - B_{\text{InfoFCWorker}}X_{\text{InfoFCWorker}}$$

Notice several features of these equations. First, each equation has a different threshold (e.g., t_1 and t_2), but all share one common slope (B). Ordinal logistic regression assumes the effect of the IVs is the same for different values of the DV. For example, information has the same effect on the odds of being dissatisfied (compared to being neutral or satisfied) as it does on the odds of being dissatisfied or neutral (compared to being satisfied). This is the *proportional odds* or *parallel regression* assumption mentioned above. You should always check this assumption, and we will discuss how to do that below. Second, notice that the slope is multiplied by a value of the IV and subtracted from, not added to, the threshold. (See Cohen et al. [2003] for another formulation of this model.)

Table 4.2 shows partial results for the ordinal logistic regression. As shown in Table 4.2, information and satisfaction are significantly related. The sign of the slope (1.139) is positive, indicating that higher values of the IV are associated with higher values of the DV. In our example, mothers who received sufficient information were more satisfied.

Table 4.2 Parameter Estimates

Parameter	B	Std. Error	95% Wald CI		Hypothesis Test			Exp(B)	95% Wald CI Exp(B)	
			Lower	Upper	Wald Chi-Square	df	Sig.		Lower	Upper
[Satisfaction = 1]	-.912	.1656	-1.237	-.588	30.359	1	.000	.402	.290	.556
[Satisfaction = 2]	.235	.1547	-.069	.538	2.299	1	.129	1.264	.934	1.712
[InfoFCWorker = 1]	1.139	.2380	.673	1.605	22.907	1	.000	3.123	1.959	4.979

From Table 4.2, the estimated ordinal logistic regression equations are:

$$L_{\text{(Dissatisfied vs. Neutral/Satisfied)}} = -.912 - (1.139)(X)$$

$$L_{\text{(Dissatisfied/Neutral vs. Satisfied)}} = .235 - (1.139)(X)$$

You can calculate the estimated values of logits, odds, and probabilities using the ordinal regression equations. For example, estimated cumulative logits for mothers who received sufficient information when ($X = 1$) are:

$$L_{\text{(Dissatisfied vs. Neutral/Satisfied)}} = -2.051 = -.912 - (1.139)(1)$$

$$L_{\text{(Dissatisfied/Neutral vs. Satisfied)}} = -.904 = .235 - (1.139)(1)$$

See Figure 4.2 for the estimated logits. As you see, logits for dissatisfied (compared to neutral or satisfied) and dissatisfied or neutral (compared to satisfied) are lower for mothers who received sufficient information. That is, mothers who received sufficient information are less likely to be dissatisfied (compared to neutral or satisfied), and they are also less likely to be dissatisfied or neutral (compared to satisfied).

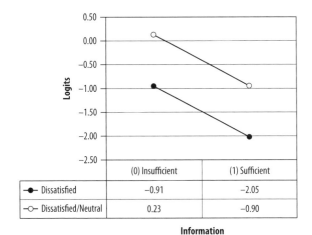

Figure 4.2 Effect of Information on Satisfaction (Logits)

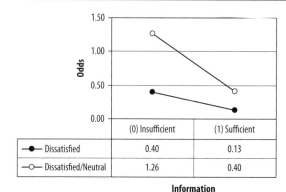

Figure 4.3 Effect of Information on Satisfaction (Odds)

Estimated cumulative odds are obtained by exponentiating the logits. For example, estimated odds for mothers who received sufficient information are:

$$Odds_{\text{(Dissatisfied vs. Neutral/Satisfied)}} = e^{-2.051} = .129$$

$$Odds_{\text{(Dissatisfied/Neutral vs. Satisfied)}} = e^{-.904} = .405$$

Figure 4.3 shows the estimated odds, demonstrating that the odds of being dissatisfied (compared to neutral or satisfied) and the odds of being dissatisfied or neutral (compared to being satisfied) are lower for mothers who received sufficient information.

Compare the odds in Figure 4.3 to those computed in Table 4.2 using the cross-tabulation and note that they are exactly the same. This will not always be the case. Ordinal logistic regression assumes that these ORs are equal and only a single common OR is estimated, as we will discuss in more detail below.

Estimated cumulative probabilities are obtained using the inverse link function. For example, estimated probabilities for mothers who received sufficient information are:

$$\hat{p}_{\text{(Dissatisfied vs. Neutral/Satisfied)}} = \frac{e^{-2.051}}{1 + e^{-2.051}} = .11$$

$$\hat{p}_{\text{(Dissatisfied/Neutral vs. Satisfied)}} = \frac{e^{-.904}}{1 + e^{-.904}} = .29$$

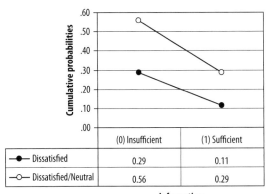

Figure 4.4 Effect of Information on Satisfaction
(Cumulative Probabilities)

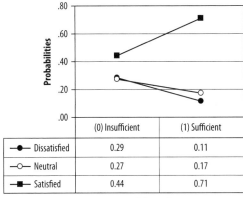

Figure 4.5 Effect of Information on Satisfaction
(Probabilities)

See Figure 4.4 for the estimated probabilities. The probabilities of being dissatisfied (compared to neutral or satisfied) and dissatisfied or neutral (compared to satisfied) are lower for mothers who received sufficient information. You might also note that the probability of being dissatisfied is very low for mothers who received sufficient information (.11).

In addition to cumulative probabilities, it can be useful to examine probabilities for individual values of the DV, and these are illustrated in Figure 4.5. The probability for a particular value of the DV is just the cumulative probability for that value minus the cumulative probability for the preceding values of the DV (Norusis, 2007). Therefore, for mothers with sufficient information, probabilities for the three values of the DV are:

$$\hat{p}_{(DV=1)} = .11 - 0 = .11$$

$$\hat{p}_{(DV=2)} = .29 - .11 = .18$$

$$\hat{p}_{(DV=3)} = 1.00 - .29 = .71$$

The cumulative probability for the highest value of the DV will always be 1.00, and the probability for the lowest value will always equal the cumulative probability for that value of the DV.

As shown in Figure 4.5, the probability of being dissatisfied or neutral is lower for mothers who received sufficient information, and the probability of being satisfied is higher. Notice that the probability of being satisfied is high for mothers who received sufficient information (.71).

In binary and multinomial logistic regression, the slope is exponentiated to obtain the OR, whereas in ordinal logistic regression, you reverse the sign of the slope before exponentiating it. So, in our example, the OR equals .31, calculated as $e^{-1.139}$. The reason for this is that in contrast to binary logistic regression, in which odds are calculated as a ratio of probabilities for higher to lower values of the DV (odds of 1 versus 0), in ordinal logistic regression it is the reverse. In our example, the odds are calculated as a ratio of the probability of being dissatisfied (i.e., 1) compared to being neutral or satisfied (2 or 3), and the ratio of the probability of dissatisfied or neutral (1 or 2) to probability of satisfied (3). So, the common OR of .32 indicates that the odds of being dissatisfied (compared to neutral or satisfied) are .32 times lesser for mothers who received sufficient information. Similarly, the odds of dissatisfied or neutral (compared to satisfied) are .32 times lesser for mothers who received sufficient information.

It is important to note in Table 4.2 that SPSS reports the exponentiated slope ($e^{1.139} = 3.123$), and the sign of the slope is not reversed before it is exponentiated ($e^{-1.139} = .320$). Therefore, either you need to compute the ORs by first reversing the sign of the slopes and then exponentiating them or you need to compute reciprocals of the ORs reported in the SPSS output (e.g., $1/3.123 = .320$).

One Quantitative Independent Variable

Both the use and interpretation of ordinal logistic regression are much the same with quantitative and categorical IVs. Let us start with a simple example to illustrate the use of ordinal logistic regression with a quantitative IV. The research question is: *Are foster mothers with more time to foster more satisfied with their foster care agencies?* The DV is the same satisfaction variable used in the previous section. The IV is scores from the ATS, converted to *z*-scores (variable name *zTime*). (Remember that using standardized scores does not change the substantive results.)

Table 4.3 shows partial results of the ordinal logistic regression, and you see a statistically significant relationship between available time and satisfaction. The sign of the slope (.281) is positive, indicating that mothers with more time are more satisfied. The OR equals .76($e^{-.281}$). This OR can be expressed in different ways. For example, you might say:

For a standard-deviation increase in available time, the odds of being dissatisfied (compared to neutral or satisfied) decrease by a factor of .76. Similarly, for a standard-deviation increase in time, the odds of being dissatisfied or neutral (compared to satisfied) decrease by a factor of .76.

You could also say:

For a standard-deviation increase in time, the odds of being dissatisfied (compared to neutral or satisfied) decrease by 24% [100(.76 − 1)]. Similarly, for a standard-deviation increase in time, the odds of being dissatisfied or neutral (compared to being satisfied) decrease by 24%.

Alternatively, given that ORs greater than 1 are easier for most people to understand, you might compute the reciprocal of the OR (1/.76 = 1.32) and say:

For a standard-deviation decrease in time, the odds of being dissatisfied (compared to neutral or satisfied) increase by a factor of 1.32. Similarly, for a standard-deviation decrease in time, the odds of being dissatisfied or neutral (compared to being satisfied) increase by a factor of 1.32.

Table 4.3 Parameter Estimates

| Parameter | B | Std. Error | 95% Wald CI | | Hypothesis Test | | | Exp(B) | 95% Wald CI Exp(B) | |
			Lower	Upper	Wald Chi-Square	df	Sig.		Lower	Upper
[Satisfaction = 1]	−1.365	.1440	−1.647	−1.083	89.879	1	.000	.255	.193	.339
[Satisfaction = 2]	−.269	.1176	−.500	−.039	5.245	1	.022	.764	.607	.962
zTime	.281	.1109	.063	.498	6.409	1	.011	1.324	1.065	1.645

Or, you could say:

For a standard-deviation decrease in available time, the odds of being dissatisfied (compared to being neutral or satisfied) increase by 32% [100(1.32 - 1)]. Similarly, for a standard-deviation decrease in time, the odds of being dissatisfied or neutral (compared to being satisfied) increase by 32%.

From Table 4.3, the estimated ordinal logistic regression equations are:

$$L_{\text{(Dissatisfied vs. Neutral/Satisfied)}} = -1.365 - (.281)(X_{z\text{Time}})$$
$$L_{\text{(Dissatisfied/Neutral vs. Satisfied)}} = -.269 - (.281)(X_{z\text{Time}})$$

Estimated values of logits, odds, and probabilities can be calculated using the ordinal regression equations. Substituting values of $-3, -2, -1, 0, 1, 2,$ and 3 for values of the IV (i.e., number of standard deviations from the mean), the estimated logits are in Figure 4.6. Logits for dissatisfied (compared to neutral or satisfied) and dissatisfied or neutral (compared to satisfied) are lower for mothers with more time. That is, mothers with more time were less likely to be dissatisfied (compared to neutral or satisfied) and less likely to be dissatisfied or neutral (compared to satisfied).

Figure 4.7 shows the estimated odds. The odds of being dissatisfied (compared to being neutral or satisfied) and the odds of being dissatisfied

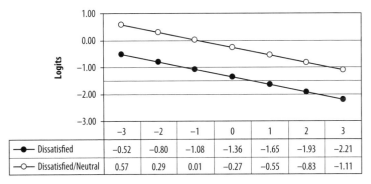

Figure 4.6 Effect of Time on Satisfaction (Logits)

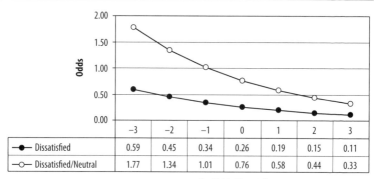

	−3	−2	−1	0	1	2	3
Dissatisfied	0.59	0.45	0.34	0.26	0.19	0.15	0.11
Dissatisfied/Neutral	1.77	1.34	1.01	0.76	0.58	0.44	0.33

Available time to foster

Figure 4.7 Effect of Time on Satisfaction (Odds)

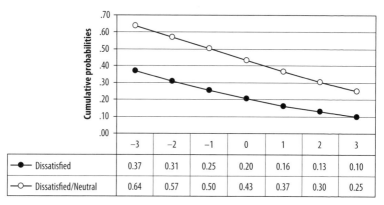

	−3	−2	−1	0	1	2	3
Dissatisfied	0.37	0.31	0.25	0.20	0.16	0.13	0.10
Dissatisfied/Neutral	0.64	0.57	0.50	0.43	0.37	0.30	0.25

Available time to foster

Figure 4.8 Effect of Time on Satisfaction (Cumulative Probabilities)

or neutral (compared to being satisfied) decrease with an increase in available time.

Figure 4.8 shows the estimated cumulative probabilities. The probability of being dissatisfied (compared to neutral or satisfied) and the probability of being dissatisfied or neutral (compared to satisfied) decrease with an increase in time. Note too that the probability of being dissatisfied or neutral is below .50 for mothers with ATS scores at or above the mean (.43, .37, .30, and .25).

You can also compute probabilities for individual values of the DV, and this is often useful. As you see in Figure 4.9, the probability of

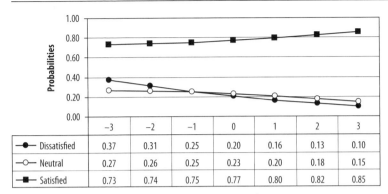

Figure 4.9 Effect of Time on Satisfaction (Probabilities)

being dissatisfied or neutral decreases with an increase in time, and the probability of being satisfied increases. You can also see that overall the probability of being satisfied is high whether ATS scores are low or high (range from .73 to .85), although the probability of being satisfied increases with an increase in time.

In this section, we illustrate change in estimated values associated with standard-deviation change in a quantitative IV by transforming the IV to z-scores. However, with quantitative IVs (as we discussed in Chapter 2) often it will also be useful to examine change associated with untransformed IVs or with mean-centered IVs (Long, 1997).

Multiple Independent Variables

Here, we build on our previous two examples in this chapter to illustrate multiple binary logistic regression. Earlier, we saw that foster mothers who received sufficient information about the role of foster care workers were more satisfied with their agencies, but it is possible that the relationship between these two variables is due to the fact that both are influenced by available time to foster (i.e., available time to foster is a "common cause" of both, and so the relationship is spurious), so the research question examined here is this: *Are foster mothers who receive sufficient information about the role of foster care workers more satisfied with their foster care agencies, controlling for available time to foster?* Data

Table 4.4 Omnibus Tests

Likelihood Ratio Chi-Square	df	Sig.
29.343	2	.000

Table 4.5 Tests of Model Effects

	Type III		
Source	Likelihood Ratio Chi-Square	df	Sig.
InfoFCWorker	22.866	1	.000
zTime	5.217	1	.022

about the role of foster care workers and available time to foster (*zTime*) are the IVs, and satisfaction with foster care agencies is the DV.

Tables 4.4, 4.5, and 4.6 show partial results of the ordinal logistic regression. The likelihood ratio χ^2 test in Table 4.4 tests the null hypothesis that $\beta_1 = \beta_2 = \beta_k = 0$ or, in our example, $\beta_{zTime} = \beta_{InfoFCWorker} = 0$, and this null hypothesis can be rejected. The likelihood ratio χ^2 tests in Table 4.5 test the null hypotheses that $\beta_{zTime} = 0$ *and* $\beta_{InfoFCWorker} = 0$. Both of these hypotheses can be rejected. These results are virtually identical to results of the Wald tests in Table 4.6.

As shown in Table 4.6, information and satisfaction are positively and significantly related when controlling for available time. We also see a positive and statistically significant relationship between time and satisfaction when controlling for information, although this is not the focus of our research question.

The OR for information is .33 ($e^{-1.116}$), which is virtually the same as we found above when we did not control for time. This OR can be expressed in different ways. For example, you might say:

The odds of being dissatisfied (compared to neutral or satisfied) are .33 times less for mothers who received sufficient information, when controlling for available time to foster. Similarly, the odds of being dissatisfied or neutral (compared to satisfied) are .33 times less for mothers who received sufficient information, when controlling for time.

The odds of being dissatisfied (compared to neutral or satisfied) are 67% lower for mothers who received sufficient information [100(.33 − 1)], when

Table 4.6 Parameter Estimates

| Parameter | B | Std. Error | 95% Wald CI | | Hypothesis Test | | | Exp(B) | 95% Wald CI Exp(B) | |
			Lower	Upper	Wald Chi-Square	df	Sig.		Lower	Upper
[Satisfaction = 1]	−.941	.1670	−1.269	−.614	31.774	1	.000	.390	.281	.541
[Satisfaction = 2]	.222	.1557	−.083	.528	2.042	1	.153	1.249	.921	1.695
zTime	.260	.1141	.036	.483	5.177	1	.023	1.296	1.037	1.621
[InfoFCWorker = 1]	1.116	.2392	.648	1.585	21.776	1	.000	3.054	1.911	4.881

controlling for time. Similarly, the odds of being dissatisfied or neutral (compared to satisfied) are 67% lower for mothers who received sufficient information [100(.33 − 1)], when controlling for time.

Given that ORs greater than 1 are easier for most people to understand, you might compute the reciprocal of the OR and say:

The odds of being dissatisfied (compared to neutral or satisfied) are 3.03 (1/.33) times greater for mothers who received insufficient information, when controlling for time. Similarly, the odds of being dissatisfied or neutral (compared to satisfied) are 3.03 (1/.33) times greater for mothers who received insufficient information, when controlling for time.

The odds of being dissatisfied (compared to neutral or satisfied) are 203% higher for mothers who received insufficient information [100(3.03 − 1)]. Similarly, the odds of being dissatisfied or neutral (compared to satisfied) are 203% higher for mothers who received insufficient information [100(3.03 − 1)].

From Table 4.6, the estimated ordinal logistic regression equations are:

$$L_{(\text{Dissatisfied vs. Neutral/Satisfied})} = -.941 - [(1.116)(X_{\text{InfoFCWorker}})$$

$$+ (.260)(X_{\text{zTime}})]$$

$$L_{(\text{Dissatisfied/Neutral vs. Satisfied})} = .222 - [(1.116)(X_{\text{InfoFCWorker}})$$

$$+ (.260)(X_{\text{zTime}})]$$

These equations can be used to compute logits, odds, ORs, and probabilities, as discussed above. To understand and present results of an ordinal logistic regression it is important to examine odds, ORs, and probabilities for substantively informative values of your IVs (e.g., insufficient and sufficient information) and for substantively important types of cases (e.g., mothers with the mean amount of available time who did and did not receive sufficient information). For continuous IVs without inherently informative substantive values, you might compute and report estimated probabilities using the mean and one or two standard deviations above and below the mean (or the 25% and 75% percentiles), fixing all other IVs at selected values (Hoffmann, 2004; Long & Freese, 2006).

Computing estimated logits, probabilities, and odds for ordinal logistic regression is relatively straightforward. Knowing what to compute and report is complicated by the potential amount of information, and of course this is compounded as the number of IVs increases. (Moreover, we know of no substitute for knowledge of the substantive area and related theory in making decisions about what to compute and present.) There is no conventional way to do this, but below we examine a few possibilities.

Odds for cases with different values of the IVs can be presented in tables or, as illustrated in Chapters 2 and 3, figures. Table 4.7 shows estimated odds for mothers who received sufficient and insufficient information for three different levels of time. From this table you can see, for example, that the odds of being dissatisfied or neutral (compared to satisfied) are especially high for mothers who received insufficient information and have relatively little time (odds = 2.10). Even for mothers with the mean amount of time, the odds of being less than satisfied (i.e., dissatisfied or neutral) are greater than the odds of being satisfied for mothers who received insufficient information (odds = 1.25).

A good place to start presenting probabilities is to examine the frequency distributions of the probabilities for all cases, basic descriptive statistics (e.g., mean, median, standard deviation, range, and interquartile range), and different types of univariate charts (histogram, boxplot, etc.). SPSS will compute estimated probabilities for each case, for each category of the DV. You can see these descriptive statistics in Table 4.8. The mean estimated probabilities for *Dissatisfied* and *Neutral* are low relative to *Satisfied*, and the variability of these probabilities is relatively low for *Neutral* and high for *Satisfied*.

Table 4.7 Estimated Odds as a Function of Available Time and Information

Information	Estimated Odds Available Time		
	−2SD	M	+2SDs
Sufficient			
Dissatisfied	.21	.13	.08
Dissatisfied/Neutral	.69	.41	.24
Insufficient			
Dissatisfied	.66	.39	.23
Dissatisfied/Neutral	2.10	1.25	.74

Table 4.8 Descriptive Statistics for Estimated Probabilities as a Function of Satisfaction

Statistic	Dissatisfied	Neutral	Satisfied
M	.21	.23	.57
Mdn	.22	.26	.52
SD	.10	.05	.15
Minimum	.07	.13	.24
Maximum	.49	.28	.80
Percentiles			
25	.11	.18	.44
50	.22	.26	.52
75	.28	.28	.71

Table 4.9 Estimated Probabilities as a Function of Available Time and Information

| | Estimated Probabilities Available Time | | |
Information	−2SD	M	+2SDs
Sufficient			
Dissatisfied	.18	.11	.07
Dissatisfied/Neutral	.41	.29	.20
Insufficient			
Dissatisfied	.40	.28	.19
Dissatisfied/Neutral	.68	.56	.43

The challenge is to summarize changes in IVs associated with changes in probabilities in the most meaningful and parsimonious way when there is no standard way to do this. This is complicated by the fact that the relationships between IVs and probabilities are not linear. For any given analysis, you should explore different ways to present the key substantive findings in tables and graphs (Long & Freese, 2006). As always, this depends in part on the subject and objectives of the study.

Probabilities for cases with different values of the IVs can be presented in tables or, as illustrated in Chapters 2 and 3, in figures. Table 4.9 shows estimated probabilities for mothers who received sufficient and insufficient information for three different levels of available time. From this table, you can see, for example, that the probability of being less than satisfied (i.e., dissatisfied or neutral) is especially high for mothers who received insufficient information and have relatively little time (.68). Even for mothers with the mean amount of time, the probability of being less than satisfied is greater than .50 for mothers who received insufficient information (.56).

Interactions and Curvilinear Relationships

Interactions and curvilinear relationships can be examined with ordinal logistic regression (Hosmer & Lemeshow, 2000; Jaccard, 2001), using the same principles and methods as you use with binary logistic regression. However, interpretation and presentation of the results are complicated by the fact that you need to consider results from more than one regression equation and, of course, this complexity increases as the number of categories of the DV increases.

Assumptions Necessary for Testing Hypotheses

Ordinal logistic regression assumes that the DV is ordinal, and this method should not be used if the order of the categories of the DV is ambiguous (e.g., type of exit from foster care ordered as reunification, adoption, or independent living). As Long and Cheng (2004) noted, a DV can be ordered differently with respect to different IVs, ordered on more than one dimension, or partially ordered. In situations where the ordinal nature of the DV is in question, data can be analyzed using multinomial logistic regression (Hosmer & Lemeshow, 2000) or using alternative regression models that do not require this assumption (Long & Freese, 2006).

Other than the assumption that the DV is ordinal, ordinal logistic regression has the same assumptions as binary logistic regression (pp. 21–28), with one addition. Ordinal logistic regression also assumes that the effect of the IVs is the same for all values of the DV. This assumption is called the *proportional odds, parallel lines, parallel slopes,* or *parallel regression assumption* (Borooah, 2002; Hardin & Hilbe, 2007; Long, 1997), and we will refer to it as the **parallel lines assumption**. The parallel lines assumption can and should be tested, and both Long (1997) and Long and Freese (2006) note that it is not unusual for it to be violated.

Consider the ordinal logistic regression equations for our example with two IVs:

$$L_{(\text{Dissatisfied vs. Neutral/Satisfied})} = t_1 - (B_{\text{InfoFCWorker}}X_{\text{InfoFCWorker}} + B_{\text{zTime}}X_{\text{zTime}})$$

$$L_{(\text{Dissatisfied/Neutral vs. Satisfied})} = t_2 - (B_{\text{InfoFCWorker}}X_{\text{InfoFCWorker}} + B_{\text{zTime}}X_{\text{zTime}})$$

Table 4.10 Test of Parallel Lines

Model	−2 Log Likelihood	Chi-Square	df	Sig.
Null Hypothesis	341.914			
General	341.559	.355	2	.838

Ordinal logistic regression assumes that $B_{InfoFCWorker}$ is the same for both equations, and B_{zTime} is the same for both equations (i.e., the slope of the lines, or in this case planes, for the two equations are parallel). If the slopes for an IV are different for different cumulative ordered categories of the DV, estimation of a common slope misrepresents the association between the IV and the DV (e.g., imagine that the sign of B_{zTime} is negative in one equation and positive in the other). So, when this assumption is violated, it is unreasonable to estimate an ordinal logistic regression model because it is unreasonable to estimate a common slope.

If the parallel lines assumption is violated, the multinomial logistic regression model could be used. However, such an analysis would not take account of the ordinal nature of the DV, and hence results might not fully address the research questions (DeMaris, 2004; Hosmer & Lemeshow, 2000).

Table 4.10 shows the SPSS output for testing the parallel lines assumption with our example with two IVs. SPSS tests the proportional odds assumption by comparing the −2 Log Likelihood for the constrained model (row labeled *Null Hypothesis*) that assumes the slopes are equal to the −2 Log Likelihood for the unconstrained model (row labeled *General)*, which allows the slopes to vary and estimates different slopes. The difference between these −2 Log Likelihood values is distributed as a chi-squared statistic, and rejection of the null hypothesis indicates that the parallel lines assumption is violated. This is a null hypothesis that you do not want to reject, because it means that the parallel lines assumption is violated (Norusis, 2007). As you can see in Table 4.10, the null hypothesis is not rejected in our example.

Model Evaluation

Methods for detecting outliers and influential observations are not well developed for ordinal logistic regression. However, you can create a set of binary DVs from the ordinal DV, run separate binary logistic regressions, and use binary logistic regression methods to detect outliers and influential observations (Hosmer & Lemeshow, 2000; Long & Freese, 2006). For our example, you could use the following SPSS syntax to create two new dichotomous variables, *SatisfactionLessThan2* and *SatisfactionLessThan3*, by recoding the original DV, *Satisfaction*, into two new variables:

    compute Satisfaction (1 = 1) (2 = 0) (3 = 0) into SatisfactionLessThan2.
    compute Satisfaction (1 = 1) (2 = 1) (3 = 0) into SatisfactionLessThan3.

SatisfactionLessThan2 equals 1 when the DV is less than 2 (i.e., when it is 1) and 0 when the DV equals 2 or 3. *SatisfactionLessThan3* equals 1 when the DV is less than 3 (i.e., when it is 1 or 2) and 0 when the DV equals 3. Notice that the new dichotomous variables correspond to the cumulative ordered categories of the DV, and the number of new dichotomous variables is one less than the number of categories of the DV.

You should construct and examine index plots for leverage values, standardized or unstandardized deviance residuals, as well as Cook's D. For example, Figure 4.10 shows the index plot of standardized deviance residuals for a binary logistic regression with *InfoFCWorker* and *zTime* as the IVs and *SatisfactionLessThan2* as the DV. No cases have markedly different values from the other cases, and no residual is less than -2 or much more than $+2$.

Multicollinearity

You examine multicollinearity the same way with ordinal logistic regression as you do with the other regression models discussed in this book. For our example with two IVs, tolerance equals .99 and the variance inflation factor equals 1.01, indicating no concern with multicollinearity.

Additional Regression Models for Ordinal Dependent Variables

In addition to ordinal logistic regression, other logistic regression models can be used with ordinal DVs (Greene, 2008; Hardin & Hilbe, 2007; Hosmer & Lemeshow, 2000; Long & Cheng, 2004; Long & Freese, 2006; Norusis, 2007). Indeed, calling the model we discuss in this chapter *the* ordinal logistic regression model is a bit misleading, because there are

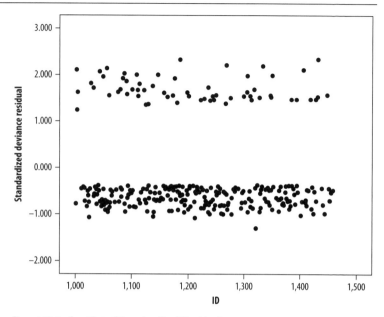

Figure 4.10 Index Plot of Standardized Residuals

other ordinal logistic regression models and the one we discuss in this chapter is, perhaps, best referred to as the *constrained cumulative logit model*. For example, the *adjacent-category logistic model* compares each value of the DV to the next higher value, the *continuation-ratio logistic model* compares each value of the DV to all lower values, and the *generalized ordered logit model* relaxes the parallel lines assumption.

In addition to ordinal regression models based on the logit link, there are regression models based on other link functions (Hardin & Hilbe, 2007; Norusis, 2007). Ordinal probit regression is the alternative most often discussed (Borooah, 2002; Hoffmann, 2004; Long & Freese, 2006). Ordinal probit regression is an extension of binary probit regression that assumes that the ordinal DV has an underlying normally-distributed latent variable. As with binary probit and logit models, the choice between the ordered probit and the logit models is largely one of convenience and discipline-specific convention, given that substantive results are generally indistinguishable (Long, 1997). Other links include the *complementary log-log link* (also known as *clog-log*), useful when higher categories are more probable, *negative log-log* link, useful when lower categories are more probable, and the *Cauchit* link, useful when the DV has a number of extreme values.

Additional Readings and Web Links

A number of books contain good chapters discussing ordinal logistic regression. These include Borooah (2002), DeMaris (2004), Hoffmann (2004), Hosmer and Lemeshow (2000), Long (1997), Long and Freese (2006), Norusis (2007), and O'Connell (2006). Several published articles also provide good examples of the application of ordinal logistic regression. For example, Cole and Eamon (2007) used ordered logistic regression to predict depressive symptoms (*none, one to three symptoms,* or *four to thirty symptoms*) in foster caregivers. IVs included income, health, childhood maltreatment, and available time to carry out responsibilities.

You might find the following Web sites useful resources for ordinal logistic regression:

http://www.stat.ubc.ca/~rollin/teach/643w04/lec/node62.html
http://teaching.sociology.ul.ie/SSS/lugano/node74.html

SPSS Instructions

Ordinal Logistic Regression (GZLM)

There are two ways to estimate ordinal logistic regression with SPSS. Let's start with SPSS *GZLM*, and then we'll turn to instructions for estimating ordinal logistic regression with SPSS *Regression*. The most important difference between these two approaches is that SPSS *Regression* provides a test of the parallel lines assumption, and SPSS *GZLM* does not.

- Start SPSS 16 and open the Chapter 4 data set.
- From the menus choose:

  Analyze
  Generalized Linear Models
  (GZLM) Generalized Linear Models. . .

Type of Model

- Click *Ordinal Logistic*.

Response

- Select an ordinal DV (e.g., *Satisfaction*), and click the arrow button to move it to *Dependent Variable*.

Predictors

- Select categorical IVs (e.g., *InfoFCWorker*), and click the arrow button to move them to *Factors*.

  - For a polytomous variable, click *Options* and click *Ascending* or *Descending* to use the last or first category, respectively, as the reference category for dummy coding. For a dichotomous variable coded as 0 and 1 typically *Descending*, should be used.

- Select quantitative IVs (e.g., *zTime*), and click the arrow button to move them to *Covariates*.

Model

- Select factors and covariates included as main effects in the model, and click the arrow button to move them to *Model*.

Note: You can also use this dialog box to create interaction terms. Click *Help* to get a description of how to do this.

Estimation

- You don't need to change default settings.

Statistics

- Click *Likelihood ratio*, listed under *Chi-Square Statistics*.
- Click *Include exponential parameter estimates*, listed under *Print*.

Estimated Marginal (EM) Means

- EM means are not available for ordinal logistic regression.

Save

- Click *Predicted value of linear predictor* to save predicted logits.
- Click *OK* to get the results.

Note: After you run the analysis save the data set, which now contains new variables that you can use to create index plots and for other purposes.

Ordinal Logistic Regression (Regression)

- Start SPSS 16 and open the Chapter 4 data set.
- From the menus choose:
  Analyze
  Regression
  Ordinal. . .
- Select an ordinal DV (e.g., *Satisfaction*), and click the arrow button to move it to *Dependent*.
- Select categorical IVs (e.g., *InfoFCWorker*), and click the arrow button to move them to *Factors*.
- Select quantitative IVs (e.g., *zTime*), and click the arrow button to move them to *Covariate(s)*.
- Click *Output,* and then click *Goodness of fit statistics, Summary statistics, Parameter estimates, Test of parallel lines,* and *Estimated response probabilities.* Click *Continue.*
- Click *OK* to get the results.

Note: After you run the analysis save the data set, which now contains new variables created by *Output.*

Excel Workbooks

The names of the following three workbooks correspond to the variables used in the associated ordinal logistic regression analyses. These workbooks show how we created the figures reported in this chapter for the associated analyses, as well as additional related figures not included.

- InfoFCWorker.xls
- zATS.xls
- zATS InfoFCWorker.xls

5

Regression with a Count Dependent Variable

Researchers spend much of their time counting things: numbers of criminal offenses, symptoms, placements, and so on. We have investigated the number of specific concerns a new mother expresses about providing care for her infant (Combs-Orme et al., 2004) and the number of children fostered or adopted (Orme et al., 2007). This chapter describes the use of Poisson and negative binomial regression to model count DVs.

Count variables indicate the number of times a particular event occurs to each case, usually within some domain of observation such as a given time period (e.g., number of hospital visits per year), population size (e.g., number of registered sex offenders per 100,000 population), or geographical area (e.g., number of divorces per county or state). Counts are whole numbers that can range from 0 through $+\infty$; social workers and those in related areas frequently conduct research in which the DV is a count.

A number of regression models are available for analyzing count DVs. This chapter first describes Poisson regression, which is the basic model upon which many other regression models for counts are based (DeMaris, 2004; Hardin & Hilbe, 2007; Hilbe, 2007; Hoffmann, 2004; Long & Freese, 2006; Norusis, 2007).

Many times the assumptions of Poisson regression are not met, and negative binomial regression is an alternative to Poisson regression with less restrictive assumptions (DeMaris, 2004; Hardin & Hilbe, 2007; Hilbe, 2007; Hoffmann, 2004; Long & Freese, 2006). Negative binomial regression has greater generality than Poisson regression, and it's the basic model on which a number of other regression models for count DVs are based (DeMaris, 2004; Hardin & Hilbe, 2007; Hilbe, 2007; Hoffmann, 2004; Long & Freese, 2006; Norusis, 2007). Therefore, after discussing Poisson regression, we will turn to a discussion of negative binomial regression.

Chapter Example

In this chapter, we will discuss and illustrate Poisson and negative binomial regression by examining variables that influence the number of foster children adopted by foster mothers. The sample includes 285 foster mothers. The number of foster children adopted is the DV (variable name *NumberAdopted*). As illustrated in Figure 5.1, the distribution is skewed positively with a large percentage of 0 values, as is common with count variables. The $M = 1.04$ ($SD = 1.53$), and the range is from 0 through 8.

We will analyze the effects of three IVs: marital status, perceived responsibility for parenting foster children, and number of years of fostering. Marital status (variable name *Married*) is a dichotomous variable coded 0 for unmarried mothers and 1 for married mothers. The sample contains 61 (21.4%) mothers who are unmarried and 224 (78.6%) who are married. Perceived responsibility for parenting foster children was measured using the Parenting subscale of the Foster Parent Role Performance Scale (FPRPS-P, variable name *ParentRole*) (Le Prohn, 1994; Rhodes, Orme, & McSurdy, 2003b). The FPRPS-P has a potential range of values from 0 through 100, with higher scores indicating a greater degree of perceived responsibility for parenting foster children. The scale has a fairly normal distribution with $M = 77.04$ ($SD = 11.27$), and it ranges from 47.83 through 100. Finally, the length of time mothers had fostered (variable name *YearsFostered*) was measured in years. It's positively skewed with $M = 7.59$ ($SD = 7.22$) and ranges from 1 through 34.

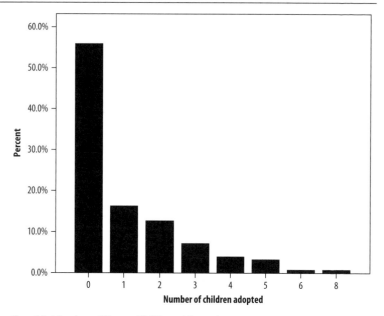

Figure 5.1   Number of Foster Children Adopted

Table 5.1   Number of Foster Children Adopted as a Function
of Marital Status

Marital Status	Mean	N	Variance
(0) No	0.754	61	1.489
(1) Yes	1.112	224	2.557
Total	1.035	285	2.344

Group Means

Let us start by examining a simple research question: *Is there a difference
in the number of foster children adopted by unmarried and married foster
mothers?* A comparison of the mean number of foster children adopted
by unmarried and married foster mothers provides a good starting point
for answering this question and for understanding Poisson and negative
binomial regression.

Table 5.1 shows descriptive statistics for the number of foster children adopted by unmarried and married mothers. The mean number
of children adopted equals 0.75 for unmarried and 1.11 for married
mothers.

You can select different ways to quantify the direction and the strength of this relationship. On average, married mothers adopted 0.36 more children ($1.112 - 0.754$), or you could say that being married increased the number of children adopted by a factor of 1.47 ($1.112/0.754$). Similarly, you could say that a one-point increase in the IV (unmarried to married) increased the mean number of children adopted by a factor of 1.47. Finally, you could say that being married increased the mean number of children adopted by 47% ($[1.112-0.754]/0.754$ or, alternatively, $100[1.47 - 1.00]$).

We have a problem with this analysis: It does not take account of the fact that number of years of fostering varied across mothers, and so opportunity to adopt foster children varied. For unmarried mothers, the mean number of years of fostering was 8.803, and for married mothers it was 7.254.

The opportunity for an event to occur is known as **exposure**. Exposure can include length of time, population size, geographical area, or other domains of interest.

If exposure is not the same for all cases, this fact must be taken into account since a higher count might simply be due to greater exposure. For example, the longer a mother fosters, the more opportunity she has to adopt foster children. Exposure can be accounted for by examining a **rate**, which is a count per unit of time (e.g., number of children adopted per year), population (e.g., number of registered sex offenders per 100,000), geographical area (e.g., number of children below the poverty line per state), or other type of exposure. A rate is calculated as:

$$\lambda = \mu/E$$

where λ (Greek letter *lambda*) is the population rate (sometimes referred to as *incidence rate*), μ (Greek letter *mu*) is the population mean for the count DV (sometimes referred to as *incidence*), and E is exposure. The estimated rates in our example are:

$$\text{rate}_{(\text{Unmarried})} = .754/8.803 = .086$$

$$\text{rate}_{(\text{Married})} = 1.112/7.254 = .153$$

On average, married mothers adopted 0.067 more children per year ($0.153 - 0.086$). You could also say that being married increased the mean yearly adoption rate by 78% [(.153 − 0.086)/0.086], a value considerably larger than when exposure was not taken into account (47%).

> What if, in our example, all mothers fostered for 1 year? In that case, the yearly adoption rates would be:
>
> $$\text{rate}_{(\text{Unmarried})} = 0.754/1.000 = 0.754$$
>
> $$\text{rate}_{(\text{Married})} = 1.112/1.000 = 1.112$$
>
> These rates are, of course, just the mean number of children adopted.

The direction and strength of the relationship between marital status and adoption rate also can be quantified using the **incidence rate ratio** (IRR), which is similar to the OR except that the response is the number of events per some unit of exposure. The IRR has a potential range from 0 through $+\infty$, and an IRR greater than 1 indicates that the numerator group has a higher incidence rate than the denominator group, while an IRR less than 1 indicates that the numerator group has a lower incidence rate than the denominator group.

In our example the IRR is:

$$IRR = \text{rate}_{(\text{Married})}/\text{rate}_{(\text{Unmarried})} = 0.153/0.086 = 1.78$$

That is, being married increased the mean yearly adoption rate by a factor of 1.78 (0.153/0.086). Also, you could say that a one-point increase in the IV (unmarried to married) increased the mean yearly adoption rate by a factor of 1.78. You can also use the IRR to compute percentage change in the rate in the same way you use the OR to compute percentage change in the odds. That is, being married increased the mean yearly adoption rate by 78% [100(1.78 − 1.00)].

Poisson Regression

This Poisson regression model can be written as (ignoring exposure for the moment, as you would do if exposure were the same for all cases, in which case $\lambda = \mu$):

$$\ln(\lambda) = \alpha + \beta_1 X_1 + \beta_2 X_2 + \ldots \beta_k X_k$$

Or, for short, it can be written as:

$$\ln(\lambda) = \eta$$

This is read as "the natural log of the rate equals the linear predictor." That is, the *log link* is the link function for the Poisson regression model.

As we discussed in previous chapters, functions of the DV, like the log of a rate, are difficult to interpret because they have no intuitive or substantive meaning. So, when you interpret and present your results it is useful to compute the inverse (or, reverse, if you will) of the estimated value. The exponential function is the inverse of the log function, as discussed in previous chapters, and with Poisson regression exponentiating the linear predictor, η, gives the rate:

$$\lambda = e^{\eta}$$

This is read as "the rate equals the exponentiated value of the linear predictor."

The estimated Poisson regression model for our example (ignoring exposure for the moment, as you would do if exposure were the same for all cases) is:

$$\ln(\text{rate}) = a + B_{\text{Married}}X_{\text{Married}}$$

The corresponding rate is:

$$\text{rate} = e^{a + B_{\text{Married}}X_{\text{Married}}}$$

One Dichotomous Independent Variable

Tables 5.2 and 5.3 show partial results of the Poisson regression. As shown in Table 5.2, the relationship between marital status and number of foster children adopted is statistically significant. The likelihood

Table 5.2 Omnibus Test

Likelihood Ratio Chi-Square	df	Sig.
6.380	1	.012

Table 5.3 Parameter Estimates

| Parameter | B | Std. Error | 95% Wald CI | | Hypothesis Test | | | Exp(B) | 95% Wald CI Exp(B) | |
			Lower	Upper	Wald Chi-Square	df	Sig.		Lower	Upper
(Intercept)	−.282	.1474	−.571	.007	3.664	1	.056	0.754	0.565	1.007
[Married = 1]	.388	.1605	.073	.703	5.846	1	.016	1.474	1.076	2.019

ratio χ^2 test in Table 5.2 tests the null hypothesis that all slopes equal 0, although in this case we have only one slope. Table 5.3 provides a Wald test for each slope, which also indicates a statistically significant relationship between marital status and number of foster children adopted.

The positive slope for marital status (.388) indicates that married mothers adopt more foster children than unmarried mothers do; a negative slope would indicate the opposite. The exponentiated value of the slope, Exp(B), indicates that being married increases the mean number of children adopted by a factor of 1.474. You could also say that being married increases the mean number of children adopted by 47.4% $[100(1.474 - 1)]$. These values are exactly what we obtained with descriptive statistics in Table 5.1 before we took account of exposure.

From Table 5.3, the estimated Poisson regression equation is:

$$\ln(\text{rate}) = -.282 + (.388)(X_{\text{Married}})$$

So, the estimated logs of the rates are:

$$\ln(\text{rate}_{(\text{Unmarried})}) = -.282 = -.282 + (.388)(0)$$
$$\ln(\text{rate}_{(\text{Married})}) = .106 = -.282 + (.388)(1)$$

The corresponding rates are:

$$\text{rate}_{(\text{Unmarried})} = e^{-.282} = .754$$
$$\text{rate}_{(\text{Married})} = e^{.106} = 1.112$$

That is, the mean number of children adopted equals 0.75 for unmarried and 1.11 for married mothers. On average, married mothers adopted 0.36 more children $(1.112 - .754)$. You could also say that being married increased the mean number of children adopted by a factor of 1.47 $(1.112/0.754)$, the exponentiated value of the slope, Exp(B), or you could say that being married increased the mean number of children adopted by 47% $[100(1.47 - 1)]$. Again, these values are exactly what we obtained with descriptive statistics in Table 5.1 before we took account of exposure.

If exposure for all mothers were the same, for example 1 year, the estimated means for unmarried and married mothers could be interpreted as yearly adoption rates. That is, for unmarried mothers, the mean number of children adopted per year would be 0.75 and for married mothers 1.11. However, exposure is different for different mothers, and we need to incorporate this fact into the Poisson regression model.

Typically, exposure is incorporated into a Poisson regression by first creating a new variable, the natural log of the exposure variable. In our example, *YearsFostered* is the exposure variable. The following SPSS syntax could be used to compute the new variable:

```
compute lnYearsFostered = ln(YearsFostered).
```

The new variable, *lnYearsFostered*, is called an **offset variable**. The log of the exposure variable is used instead of the exposure variable itself so that exposure will be on the log scale, just as other values of the linear predictor, η, are on the log scale. Note that the exposure variable must be greater than 0; that is, there must be some opportunity for the event to occur, and logs of values less than or equal to 0 are undefined.

Tables 5.4 and 5.5 show partial results of the Poisson regression incorporating the offset variable, *lnYearsFostered*. The relationship between marital status and number of children adopted per year is statistically significant as indicated by the likelihood ratio χ^2 test and the Wald test.

The positive slope for marital status (.582) indicates that the yearly adoption rate is higher for married mothers. In fact, the relationship between adoption rate and marital status is stronger (the slope is larger), when exposure is considered than when it is not. The exponentiated value of the slope, Exp(B), indicates that being married increases the mean yearly adoption rate by a factor of 1.79; this is the IRR. Instead, you could say that a one-point increase in the IV (unmarried to married) increases the mean yearly adoption rate by a factor of 1.79, or that being married increases the mean yearly adoption rate by 79% [$100(1.79 - 1)$]. These values are exactly (given rounding error) what we obtained with descriptive statistics presented above when we took account of exposure.

Table 5.4 Omnibus Test

Likelihood Ratio Chi-Square	df	Sig.
14.940	1	.000

Table 5.5 Parameter Estimates

| Parameter | B | Std. Error | 95% Wald CI | | Hypothesis Test | | | Exp(B) | 95% Wald CI Exp(B) | |
			Lower	Upper	Wald Chi-Square	df	Sig.		Lower	Upper
(Intercept)	−2.457	.1474	−2.746	−2.168	277.776	1	.000	0.086	0.064	0.114
[Married = 1]	.582	.1605	.267	.896	13.131	1	.000	1.789	1.306	2.450

From Table 5.5, the estimated Poisson regression equation is:

$$\ln(\text{rate}) = a + B_{\text{Married}} X_{\text{Married}}$$

So, the estimated log of the rates is:

$$\ln(\text{rate}_{(\text{Unmarried})}) = -2.457 = -2.457 + (.582)(0)$$
$$\ln(\text{rate}_{(\text{Married})}) = -1.875 = -2.457 + (.582)(1)$$

The corresponding rates are:

$$\text{rate}_{(\text{Unmarried})} = e^{-2.457} = .086$$
$$\text{rate}_{(\text{Married})} = e^{-1.875} = .153$$

These values are exactly what we obtained with descriptive statistics (presented above) when we accounted for exposure.

When you do not include an offset variable in your regression model, as might be the situation if exposure is the same for all cases, the mean count is a rate. So, for example, if only mothers who fostered for 1 year were included in the sample, the mean count would be the yearly adoption rate.

When an offset variable is included in Poisson regression, the estimated rate for a particular case is computed by first calculating the estimated log of the rate. In our example:

$$\ln(\text{rate}) = a + B_{\text{Married}} X_{\text{Married}} + \ln(E)$$

Then, the value of the linear predictor is exponentiated to obtain the estimated rate:

$$\text{rate} = e^{a + B_{\text{Married}} X_{\text{Married}} + \ln(E)}$$

In both of these equations note that values of $\ln(E)$ are computed for each case, and may be different for each case. For example, for mothers who fostered for 2 years, $\ln(E) = \ln(2) = .69$. Finally, notice that the offset term in the regression equation [$\ln(E)$] does not have an associated slope coefficient (i.e., β is set to a value of 1).

Table 5.6 Omnibus Test

Likelihood Ratio Chi-Square	df	Sig.
10.272	1	.001

One Quantitative Independent Variable

The use and interpretation of Poisson regression is much the same with quantitative and categorical IVs. We will start with a simple example to illustrate Poisson regression with a quantitative IV. The research question is this: *Do foster mothers who feel a greater responsibility to parent foster children adopt more foster children?* As the IV, we will use scores from the Parenting subscale of the Foster Parent Role Performance Scale, transformed to *z*-scores (variable name *zParentRole*). We will include *lnYearsFostered* as the offset variable.

Tables 5.6 and 5.7 show partial results of the Poisson regression. The relationship between parenting responsibility and yearly adoption rate is statistically significant as indicated by the likelihood ratio χ^2 test and the Wald tests.

The slope (.184) is positive, and the IRR (1.202) is greater than 1, indicating a positive relationship between parenting responsibility and yearly adoption rate. That is, for every one standard-deviation increase in parenting responsibility, the mean yearly adoption rate increases by a factor of 1.20. (Or, for every two standard-deviation increase in parenting responsibility, the yearly adoption rate increases by a factor of 1.44 [i.e., $e^{(2)(.184)}$].) Finally, you could say that for every one standard-deviation increase in parenting responsibility, the yearly adoption rate increased by 20% $[100(1.20 - 1.00)]$.

From Table 5.7, the estimated Poisson regression equation is:

$$\ln(\text{rate}) = a + B_{zParentRole}X_{zParentRole}$$

So, for example, mothers with the mean value of parenting responsibility (i.e., when *zParentRole* = 0) is:

$$\ln(\text{rate}) = -2.008 = -2.008 + (.184)(0)$$

The corresponding rate is:

$$\text{rate} = e^{-2.008} = .134$$

Table 5.7 Parameter Estimates

| Parameter | B | Std. Error | 95% Wald CI | | Hypothesis Test | | | Exp(B) | 95% Wald CI Exp(B) | |
			Lower	Upper	Wald Chi-Square	df	Sig.		Lower	Upper
(Intercept)	−2.008	.0592	−2.123	−1.892	1151.808	1	.000	0.134	0.120	0.151
zParentRole	.184	.0580	.070	.297	10.045	1	.002	1.202	1.073	1.346

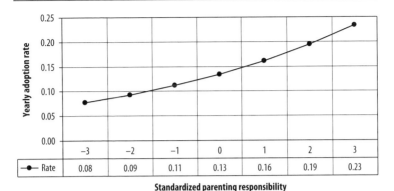

	−3	−2	−1	0	1	2	3
●— Rate	0.08	0.09	0.11	0.13	0.16	0.19	0.23

Standardized parenting responsibility

Figure 5.2   Effect of Standardized Parenting Responsibility on Adoption Rate

Figure 5.2 shows the relationship between *zParentRole* and yearly adoption rate. Note that 0 represents the mean value of parenting responsibility; −1, −2, and −3 indicate the number of standard deviations below the mean; and 1, 2, and 3 indicate the number of standard deviations above the mean. Thus, for example, the estimated mean yearly adoption rate for mothers with the mean value of parenting responsibility is 0.13.

Multiple Independent Variables

Now we build on our previous two examples in this chapter to illustrate Poisson regression with multiple IVs. Earlier, we saw that the mean yearly adoption rate was greater for mothers who were married and for mothers who took more responsibility for parenting. It might be that the relationship between parenting responsibility and yearly adoption rate is due to the fact that both are influenced by marital status (i.e., marital status is a "common cause" of both, and so the relationship is spurious). Therefore, the research question examined here is this: *Do foster mothers who take more responsibility for parenting adopt more foster children per year, controlling for marital status?*

Marital status and parenting responsibility were included in the regression model, and *lnYearsFostered* was included as the offset variable. We show partial results of this analysis in Tables 5.8, 5.9, and 5.10.

The likelihood ratio χ^2 test in Table 5.8 tests the null hypothesis that $\beta_1 = \beta_2 = \beta_k = 0$ or, in our example, $\beta_{\text{zParentRole}} = \beta_{\text{Married}} = 0$. As you

Table 5.8 Omnibus Test

Likelihood Ratio Chi-Square	df	Sig.
26.792	2	.000

Table 5.9 Tests of Model Effects

	Type III		
Source	Likelihood Ratio Chi-Square	df	Sig.
(Intercept)	2200.743	1	.000
zParentRole	11.853	1	.001
Married	16.520	1	.000

can see, we can reject the null hypothesis. The likelihood ratio χ^2 tests in Table 5.9 test the null hypotheses that $\beta_{zParentRole} = 0$ and $\beta_{Married} = 0$. Both of these hypotheses can be rejected, and these results are identical to results of the Wald tests shown in Table 5.10.

As shown in Table 5.10, the slope for parenting responsibility (.198) is positive, and the IRR (1.22) is greater than 1, indicating a positive relationship between parenting responsibility and yearly adoption rate, when controlling for marital status. That is, for every one standard-deviation increase in parenting responsibility, the mean yearly adoption rate increased by a factor of 1.22, when controlling for marital status. (Or, for every two standard-deviation increase in parenting responsibility, the mean yearly adoption rate increased by a factor of 1.49 [i.e., $e^{(2)(.198)}$], when controlling for marital status.) Finally, you could say that for every one standard-deviation increase in parenting responsibility, the mean yearly adoption rate increased by 22% [$100(1.22 - 1.00)$], when controlling for marital status. This percentage increase is virtually the same as we found above (20%), when we did not control for marital status.

Although our substantive interest here is in the effect of parenting responsibility on adoption rate when controlling for marital status, we can also interpret the results for marital status. The slope for marital status (.611) is positive, and the IRR (1.842) is greater than 1. The IRR indicates that being married increased the mean yearly adoption rate by a factor of 1.84, when controlling for parenting responsibility. Or, you could say that a one-point increase in the IV (unmarried to married)

Table 5.10 Parameter Estimates

| Parameter | B | Std. Error | 95% Wald CI | | Hypothesis Test | | | Exp(B) | 95% Wald CI Exp(B) | |
			Lower	Upper	Wald Chi-Square	df	Sig.		Lower	Upper
(Intercept)	−2.498	.1485	−2.789	−2.207	282.867	1	.000	.082	0.062	0.110
zParentRole	.198	.0582	.084	.312	11.576	1	.001	1.219	1.088	1.366
[Married = 1]	.611	.1607	.296	.926	14.443	1	.000	1.842	1.344	2.524

increased the mean yearly adoption rate by a factor of 1.84, when controlling for parenting responsibility. Finally, you could say that being married increased the mean yearly adoption rate by 84% $[100(1.84-1.00)]$, when controlling for parenting responsibility.

From Table 5.10, the estimated Poisson regression equation is:

$$\ln(\text{rate}) = a + B_{\text{Married}}X_{\text{Married}} + B_{z\text{ParentRole}}X_{z\text{ParentRole}}$$

So, for example, for unmarried mothers (married $= 0$) with the mean value of parenting responsibility (i.e., $z\text{ParentRole} = 0$):

$$\ln(\text{rate}_{\text{Unmarried}}) = -2.498 = -2.498 + (.611)(0) + (.198)(0)$$

The corresponding rate is:

$$\text{rate} = e^{-2.498} = .082$$

That is, the estimated mean yearly adoption rate for unmarried mothers with the mean value of parenting responsibility is .08.

To think about the best way to present estimated rates, examine their frequency distributions, basic descriptive statistics (e.g., mean, median, standard deviation, range, and interquartile range), and different types of univariate charts (histogram, boxplot, etc.). SPSS will compute an expected count for each case and save these counts as a new variable, so you do not need to compute these manually. In the current example, descriptive statistics for estimated rates are: $M = .14$, $Mdn = .14$, $SD = .04$, range $= .05 - .23$, and interquartile range $= .11 - .17$.

The challenge with Poisson regression, as with all regression models discussed in this book, is to summarize changes in IVs associated with changes in rates in the most meaningful and parsimonious way, in the absence of a standard way to do this. This is further complicated by the fact that the relationship between IVs and rates is not linear. For any given analysis, you should explore different ways to present key substantive findings in tables or graphs. Again, this depends in part on the subject and objectives of the study.

Rates for cases with different values of IVs can be presented in tables. Table 5.11 shows estimated rates for unmarried and married mothers with three different levels of parenting responsibility. At each level of

Table 5.11 Estimated Adoption Rate as a Function of Parenting Responsibility and Marital Status

| Marital Status | Estimated Adoption Rate Parenting Responsibility | | |
	$M - 2SD$	M	$M + 2SD$
Unmarried	.06	.08	.12
Married	.10	.15	.23

parenting responsibility, being married increases the mean yearly adoption rate. Also, you might note that the lowest mean yearly adoption rate (.06) is for unmarried mothers two standard deviations below the mean for parenting responsibility, and the highest (.23) is for married mothers two standard deviations above the mean for parenting responsibility. That is, the mean yearly adoption rate increased by a factor of 3.83 (IRR = .23/.06) or, stated another way, by 283% [100(3.83 − 1.00)].

In addition to presenting rates in tables, it is often useful to present rates in graphic form, such as Figure 5.3. The larger the number of IVs though, the more difficult this becomes, and a limited number of IVs can be represented meaningfully on a single graph. One way to do this is to plot the relationship of one IV from its minimum to maximum value, while all other variables are fixed at their mean (or, for dichotomous variables, 0 or 1). Another strategy is to estimate rates for selected sets of values of IVs that correspond to ideal or typical types in the population (e.g., unmarried mothers with the mean for parenting responsibility).

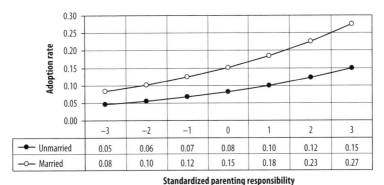

Figure 5.3 Effect of Standardized Parenting Responsibility and Marital Status on Adoption Rate

Assumptions Necessary for Testing Hypotheses

In addition to the assumptions we discussed in Chapter 1 (pp. 21–28), Poisson regression has two additional assumptions. First, it assumes that the variance equals the mean; this situation is known as **equidispersion**. *Underdispersion* occurs when the variance is smaller than the mean. The Poisson model rarely fits in practice because in most cases the variance is greater than the mean, a situation known as *overdispersion*. Typically, when overdispersion occurs standard errors are inflated and, consequently, *p* values are spuriously low. Consequently, overdispersed Poisson models may lead us to believe that IVs are statistically significant when in fact they are not (Hilbe, 2007).

All the regression models discussed in this book are based on the assumption that observations are independent of one another. Poisson regression also assumes that events for individuals are independent. That is, for an individual the occurrence of an event does not influence the occurrence of later events. For example, we assume that the fact that a person adopts a child does not make the likelihood of future adoptions more or less likely. Sometimes the violation of this assumption is referred to as *state dependence* or *contagion* (Cohen et al., 2003).

Overdispersion can result from contagion, as well as from other reasons. Hilbe (2007) provides an excellent discussion of this issue, differentiating between *apparent* and *real* overdispersion. Apparent overdispersion can occur as a result of many of the factors we discussed in Chapter 1, including, for example, outliers and the exclusion of relevant IVs, interaction terms, or curvilinear terms. The resolution of these problems may eliminate overdispersion, and these issues should be considered before you assume that overdispersion is real and proceed to use a regression model designed to accommodate overdispersion (e.g., negative binomial regression).

The test for overdispersion involves estimating a negative binomial regression, which we'll discuss below. Negative binomial regression adds an *ancillary parameter* that allows overdispersion (but not underdispersion), and this parameter is directly related to the amount of overdispersion. If the data are not overdispersed, the ancillary parameter equals 0. (Poisson regression can be considered a negative binomial regression with an ancillary parameter of 0.) Larger values of the ancillary parameter indicate more overdispersion; in practice, values typically range from

Table 5.12 Lagrange Multiplier Test

	z	Significance (by Alternative Hypothesis)		
		Parameter < 0	Parameter > 0	Non-directional
Ancillary Parameter	1.902	.971	.029	.057

0 to about 4 (Hilbe, 2007). SPSS provides a *Lagrange Multiplier test* of the null hypothesis that the ancillary parameter equals 0. Rejection of this null hypothesis indicates overdispersion.

Table 5.12 shows results of the Lagrange Multiplier test for the model with *Married* and *zParentRole*. The null hypothesis that the ancillary parameter is greater than 0 (i.e., overdispersion) can be rejected— indicating the presence of statistically significant overdispersion.

When you use this method, you should also construct index plots for leverage values, standardized or unstandardized deviance residuals, and Cook's D. For example, Figure 5.4 shows the index plot of standardized deviance residuals for our Poisson regression with *Married* and

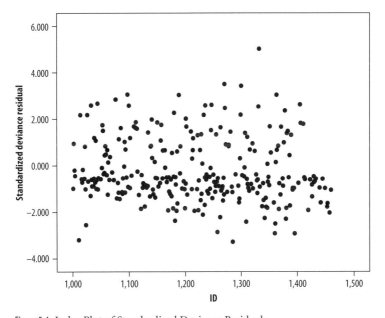

Figure 5.4 Index Plot of Standardized Deviance Residuals

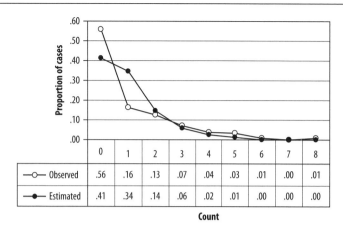

Figure 5.5 Observed versus Estimated Proportion of Cases

zParentRole as the IVs, and *lnYearsFostered* as the offset variable. Nine cases (3%) have values below −3 or above +3, and one case in particular is markedly different and especially large. This case is a married mother who has about the mean value of parenting responsibility and has fostered for 1 year but has adopted five foster children. It might be useful to rerun the analysis without this case and see whether the results change substantially. (When we excluded this case, results were virtually identical to the original results.)

It can also be useful to graph and compare observed and estimated counts. As shown in Figure 5.5, the estimated proportion of mothers who did not adopt any foster children is notably less than the actual proportion, and the estimated proportion of mothers who adopted one foster child is notably higher than the actual proportion. For counts of two and above, the estimated and actual distributions are similar. The situation where the actual number of zeros is greater than the estimated number is known as **zero-inflation**, and variations of both Poisson and negative binomial regression are designed to handle this situation (Hilbe, 2007).

Multicollinearity

The examination of multicollinearity is conducted in the same way with Poisson and negative binomial regression as with other regression models discussed in this book. For our example with two IVs, tolerance equals

.99, and the variance inflation factor equals 1.01, indicating no concern with multicollinearity.

Negative Binomial Regression

Negative binomial regression is an extension of Poisson regression that allows overdispersion (but not underdispersion). It is the standard method used to model overdispersed Poisson data. Given that overdispersion is the norm, the negative binomial regression model has more generality than the Poisson model (Hilbe, 2007).

Our focus here will be on the basic negative binomial regression model (sometimes referred to as *NB-2*). However, it is important to note that there are a number of extensions of this basic model, just as there are of the basic Poisson model, and we will discuss some of these extensions briefly at the end of this chapter.

Negative binomial regression has much in common with Poisson regression. Methods for testing the overall model, quantifying and interpreting the effects of IVs, incorporating exposure variables, estimating rates, testing interactions and curvilinear effects, testing assumptions, and quantifying multicollinearity are the same. We begin below by estimating and interpreting results of a negative binomial regression analysis of the multiple IV Poisson model we discussed above.

Multiple Independent Variables

Marital status and parenting responsibility were included in the regression model, and *lnYearsFostered* was included as the offset variable. You can see partial results of this analysis in Tables 5.13, 5.14, and 5.15.

As shown in Table 5.13, you can reject the null hypothesis that the slopes for the two IVs equal 0. In Tables 5.14 and 5.15, you can see that both *Married* and *zParentRole* are statistically significant.

As shown in Table 5.15, the slope for parenting responsibility (.227) is positive, and the IRR (1.254) is greater than 1, indicating a positive

Table 5.13 Omnibus Test

Likelihood Ratio Chi-Square	df	Sig.
8.668	2	.013

Table 5.14 Tests of Model Effects

Source	Type III		
	Likelihood Ratio Chi-Square	df	Sig.
(Intercept)	109.483	1	.000
Married	4.710	1	.030
zParentRole	4.854	1	.028

relationship between parenting responsibility and yearly adoption rate, controlling for marital status. That is, for every one standard-deviation increase in parenting responsibility, the mean yearly adoption rate increased by a factor of 1.25, controlling for marital status. Finally, you could say that for every one standard-deviation increase in parenting responsibility, the mean yearly adoption rate increased by 25% [100(1.25 − 1.00)], controlling for marital status. This percentage increase is slightly higher than the one we found with Poisson regression (22%).

Although our substantive interest here is in the effect of parenting responsibility on adoption rate controlling for marital status, we can also interpret the results for marital status. The slope for marital status (.565) is positive, and the IRR (1.760) is greater than 1. The IRR indicates that being married increased the mean yearly adoption rate by a factor of 1.76, when controlling for parenting responsibility. You could also say that a one-point increase in the IV (unmarried to married) increased the mean yearly adoption rate by a factor of 1.76, when controlling for parenting responsibility. Finally, you could say that being married increased the mean yearly adoption rate by 76% (100[1.76 − 1.00]), when controlling for parenting responsibility. This percentage increase is lower than the one we found with Poisson regression (84%).

The adoption rate is estimated by first estimating the log of the rate. So, for example, for unmarried mothers (*Married* = 0) with the mean value of parenting responsibility (i.e., when *zParentRole* = 0) the estimated log of the rate is:

$$\ln(\text{rate}_{\text{Unmarried}}) = -2.256 = -2.256 + (.565)(0) + (.227)(0)$$

The corresponding rate is:

$$\text{rate} = e^{-2.256} = .10$$

Table 5.15 Parameter Estimates

| Parameter | B | Std. Error | 95% Wald CI | | Hypothesis Test | | | Exp(B) | 95% Wald CI Exp(B) | |
			Lower	Upper	Wald Chi-Square	df	Sig.		Lower	Upper
(Intercept)	−2.256	.2337	−2.714	−1.798	93.216	1	.000	0.105	0.066	0.166
[Married = 1]	.565	.2568	.062	1.068	4.845	1	.028	1.760	1.064	2.911
zParentRole	.227	.1022	.026	.427	4.917	1	.027	1.254	1.027	1.532

Table 5.16 Estimated Adoption Rate as a Function of
Parenting Responsibility and Marital Status

	Estimated Adoption Rate Parenting Responsibility		
Marital Status	$M - 2SD$	M	$M + 2SD$
Unmarried	.07	.10	.16
Married	.12	.18	.29

This estimated yearly adoption rate is slightly higher than the rate we found with Poisson regression (.08).

As with Poisson regression, rates for cases with different values of IVs can be presented in tables. Table 5.16 shows estimated rates for unmarried and married mothers with three different levels of parenting responsibility. At each level of parenting responsibility, being married increases the mean yearly adoption rate. Also, you might note that the lowest mean yearly adoption rate (.07) is for unmarried mothers two standard deviations below the mean on parenting responsibility, and the highest (.29) is for married mothers two standard deviations above the mean on parenting responsibility. That is, the mean yearly adoption rate increased by a factor of 4.14 (IRR = .29/.07) or, stated another way, by 314% [100(4.14 − 1.00)].

In addition to presenting rates in tables, it is often useful to present rates in graphic form, such as Figure 5.6. The larger the number of IVs, of course, the more difficult this becomes, and only a limited number of IVs can be represented meaningfully on a single graph.

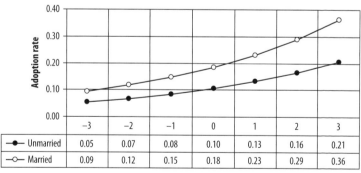

Figure 5.6 Effect of Standardized Parenting Responsibility and Marital Status on Adoption Rate

Interactions and Curvilinear Relationships

Curvilinear relationships and interactions are tested with negative binomial (and Poisson) regression in much the same way as with linear regression. However, both types of relationships are a bit more work to present and interpret, given the nonlinear relationship between the IVs and the rates.

Curvilinear Relationships

One assumption of negative binomial and Poisson regression is that the relationship between the linear combination of IVs (i.e., $\alpha + \beta_1 X_1 + \beta_2 X_2 + \ldots \beta_k X_k$, symbolized by η) and the log of the rate, $\ln(\lambda)$, is linear.

Suppose we hypothesize that responsibility for parenting positively influences adoption rates, but only up to a certain point, beyond which it has no additional effect. This is an example of a *quadratic* relationship, and oftentimes such relationships are of theoretical interest.

First create two new variables: (1) parenting responsibility (centered or transformed to z-scores, which are centered scores divided by the standard deviation—we will use z-scores) (*zParentRole*); and (2) parenting responsibility z-scores squared (*zParentRole2*). Then, enter *zParentRole* and *zParentRole2* into the regression equation, along with *lnYearsFostered* as the offset variable. If *zParentRole2* is statistically significant you conclude that a curvilinear (quadratic) relationship exists and proceed to describe the form of this relationship. If not, reestimate the model without this curvilinear term and interpret results of the "reduced" model. Partial results of this analysis shown in Table 5.17 indicate no statistically significant relationship between *zParentRole2* and adoption rate.

If the relationship between *zParentRole2* and adoption rate were statistically significant, a useful way to understand and depict the form of the curvilinear relationship would be to create a graph with *zParentRole* (not *zParentRole2*) on the horizontal axis and estimated values of the yearly adoption rate on the vertical axis. As shown in Figure 5.7, parenting responsibility has a positive relationship with yearly adoption rate up to about one standard deviation above the mean, and then the direction of the relationship is reversed slightly. However, this curvilinear relationship is not statistically significant, so normally you would not construct and interpret these graphs; we have done this for illustrative purposes.

Table 5.17 Parameter Estimates

| Parameter | B | Std. Error | 95% Wald CI | | Hypothesis Test | | | Exp(B) | 95% Wald CI Exp(B) | |
			Lower	Upper	Wald Chi-Square	df	Sig.		Lower	Upper
(Intercept)	−1.653	.1303	−1.908	−1.398	160.963	1	.000	.191	0.148	0.247
zParentRole	.196	.1024	−.004	.397	3.680	1	.055	1.217	0.996	1.488
zParentRole2	−.138	.0829	−.300	.025	2.750	1	.097	.871	0.741	1.025

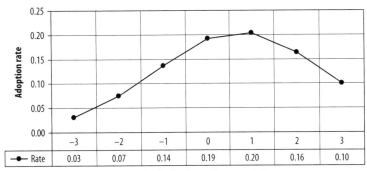

	−3	−2	−1	0	1	2	3
Rate	0.03	0.07	0.14	0.19	0.20	0.16	0.10

Standardized parenting responsibility

Figure 5.7 Curvilinear Relationship Between Standardized Parenting Responsibility and Adoption Rate

Interactions

As discussed in Chapter 1, an interaction occurs when the effect of one IV (*focal* variable) is conditional on the values of one or more other IVs (*moderator* variable). The focal variable is the IV whose effect on the DV is thought to vary as a function of the moderator variable.

For example, suppose you hypothesize that the effect of parenting responsibility (the *focal* variable) on the yearly adoption rate is different for unmarried and married mothers (marital status is the *moderator* variable). It may be that parenting responsibility has a relatively large influence on the yearly adoption rate for unmarried mothers, but less of an effect for married mothers.

First create two new variables: (1) parenting responsibility (centered or transformed to *z*-scores, which are centered scores divided by the standard deviation—we use *z*-scores here) (*zParentRole*); and (2) parenting responsibility *z*-scores multiplied by marital status (*zParentRoleXMarital*). Then, enter *zParentRole*, *married*, and *zParentRoleXMarital* into the regression equation, along with *lnYearsFostered* as the offset variable. If *zParentRoleXMarital* is statistically significant, you conclude that an interaction exists, and you describe the form of this relationship. If not, reestimate the model without this interaction term and interpret results of the "reduced" model. Partial results of this analysis in Table 5.18 indicate no statistically significant interaction.

If the interaction were statistically significant, it would be useful to create a graph with *zParentRole* on the horizontal axis, the estimated log

Table 5.18 Parameter Estimates

Parameter	B	Std. Error	95% Wald CI		Hypothesis Test			Exp(B)	95% Wald CI Exp(B)	
			Lower	Upper	Wald Chi-Square	df	Sig.		Lower	Upper
(Intercept)	−2.270	.2433	−2.747	−1.793	87.036	1	.000	.103	0.064	0.166
[Married = 1]	.579	.2659	.058	1.100	4.743	1	.029	1.784	1.060	3.005
zParentRole	.270	.2345	−.190	.730	1.326	1	.250	1.310	.827	2.075
zParentRole X Marital	−.054	.2606	−.565	.457	.043	1	.837	.948	.569	1.579

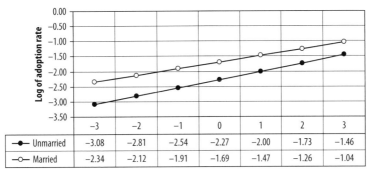

Figure 5.8 Effect of Standardized Parenting Responsibility on the log of the Adoption Rate Moderated by Marital Status

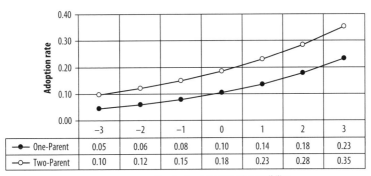

Figure 5.9 Effect of Standardized Parenting Responsibility on Adoption Rate Moderated by Marital Status

of the adoption rate (or the adoption rate itself) on the vertical axis, and separate lines representing the relationships between parenting responsibility and adoption rate for unmarried and married mothers. The graphs for this example are in Figures 5.8 and 5.9. In the absence of an interaction, the separate lines for unmarried and married mothers will be parallel for the plot of the log of the rate, but not necessarily for the rate, and the IRR relating parenting responsibility to the adoption rate will be the same regardless of marital status. Visually, the slope of the regression line is slightly steeper for unmarried mothers, as shown in Figure 5.8, implying that the effect of parenting responsibility is stronger for unmarried mothers. However, this interaction is not statistically significant and so normally you would not construct and interpret these graphs; again, we have done this for illustrative purposes.

Assumptions Necessary for Testing Hypotheses

In addition to the assumptions we discussed in Chapter 1 (pp. 21–28), overdispersion can also be a problem with negative binomial regression. Although negative binomial regression is a standard way to account for certain types of overdispersed Poisson data, and the basic negative binomial model may be sufficient to account for this overdispersion, negative binomial regression does not account for all sources of overdispersion. Hilbe (2007) provides a detailed discussion of these issues and extensions of the basic negative binomial regression model for these situations.

Index plots for leverage values, standardized or unstandardized deviance residuals, and Cook's D should be constructed and examined when you use negative binomial regression. It can also be useful to graph and compare observed and estimated counts as shown in Figure 5.5.

Additional Regression Models for Count Dependent Variables

Hilbe (2007), Hardin and Hilbe (2007), Greene (2008), and Long and Freese (2006) describe a number of extensions to the basic Poisson and negative binomial models, but SPSS 16 does not allow you to estimate most of these models. LIMDEP/NLOGIT (http://www.limdep.com/) is an especially versatile program for estimating a wide range of regression models for counts. STATA also allows you to estimate a number of these count models (Hardin & Hilbe, 2007; Long & Freese, 2006).

The negative binomial model is not appropriate when data are underdispersed. An extension of the Poisson model known as the *generalized Poisson model* can be used when data are under- or overdispersed. Hilbe (2007) predicts that this will become a well-used model one day.

In some data, you will find more zeros than are estimated by the model, as illustrated in Figure 5.8. This can occur, for example, with a mix of two processes in the count variable, one that generates only zero counts, and another that generates both zero and positive counts. For example, some parents might not adopt because they are not interested in adopting (a process that generates only zero counts), and some parents might want to adopt but have not had the opportunity (a process that generates both zero and positive counts). Extensions of the Poisson and negative binomial models known as *zero-inflated* Poisson and negative binomial models are appropriate for this situation, and the class of models known as *Hurdle models* can also be used (Greene, 2008; Hilbe, 2007).

Both the basic Poisson and the negative binomial models assume the possibility of zero counts, even if they do not exist in the data. In situations where zero counts are excluded (e.g., only mothers who have adopted one or more children are included in the sample), you can use an extension of the negative binomial model known as the *zero-truncated* negative binomial model. Also, there are extensions of the Poisson and negative binomial models designed to estimate models for more general forms of **truncation** (i.e., exclusion of cases from the population of interest based on characteristics of the DV) (Greene, 2008; Hilbe, 2007).

Poisson and negative binomial models also assume that the DV is not censored. Consider a study of the number of contacts between foster children and their biological parents. You might measure the number of contacts per month as 0, 1, 2, or *3 or more*. In this case, the values are *censored* at the top. That is, **censored variables** are variables whose values are known over some range, but are unknown beyond a certain value because they were recorded or collected only up (or down) to a certain value. Variations of the Poisson and negative binomial models exist to model DVs that are censored from above or below (Greene, 2008; Hilbe, 2007).

Additional Readings and Web Links

Hilbe (2007) provides a recent comprehensive text covering negative binomial, Poisson, and many related models. A number of books also contain good discussions of Poisson and negative binomial regression. These include Cohen et al. (2003), DeMaris (2004), Dunteman and Ho (2006), Fox (2008), Hardin and Hilbe (2007), Hoffmann (2004), Long (1997), and Long and Freese (2006).

Several published articles provide good examples of the application of Poisson regression. For example, Leslie et al. (2000) employed the method to model outpatient mental health service use (number of outpatient visits, the DV) by foster children. IVs included age, race/ethnicity, gender, maltreatment history, placement pattern, and behavior problems. Since children were in care for varying lengths of time, length of time in care was used to control for exposure.

Barth et al. (2007) examined predictors of the number of placement moves during the first 36 months of out-of-home placement. Two separate Poisson regression models tested the effects of depression, living with siblings, and other variables on number of moves for children with and without emotional disorders.

You can also find a number of published articles that provide good examples of the application of negative binomial regression. For example, Diwan, Jonnalagadda, and Balaswamy (2004) used negative binomial regression because their DVs (indicators of positive and negative affect among older Asian Indian immigrants) were overdispersed. IVs included personal characteristics, stressful life events, personal resources, and social support.

See also Smokowski, Mann, Reynolds, and Fraser (2004), who used the method to predict counts of depressive symptoms and juvenile arrests among adolescents who were part of the Chicago Longitudinal Study. IVs included a number of risk factors collected in early and middle childhood.

You might find the following Web sites useful resources for Poisson and negative binomial regression:

http://www.stat.psu.edu/~jglenn/stat504/07_poisson/
    04_poisson_model.htm
http://www.uky.edu/ComputingCenter/SSTARS/P_NB_1.htm
http://www.uky.edu/ComputingCenter/SSTARS/P_NB_3.htm

SPSS Instructions

Poisson and Negative Binomial Regression (GZLM)

- Start SPSS 16 and open the Chapter 5 data set.
- From the menus choose:
  Analyze
  Generalized Linear Models
  (GZLM) Generalized Linear Models...

Type of Model

- Click *Custom*.

  - Select *Negative binomial* from the *Distribution* drop-down box.
  - Select *Log* from the *Link function* drop-down box.
  - For Poisson regression, click *Specify value* and enter 0 for the value. For negative binomial regression, click *Estimate value*.

Note: A negative binomial regression with the ancillary parameter set to 0 is a Poisson regression. The advantage of estimating a Poisson regression this way, instead of clicking Poisson loglinear, is that you can obtain the test of overdispersion.

Response

- Select a count DV (e.g., *NumberAdopted*), and click the arrow button to move it to *Dependent Variable*.

Predictors

- Select categorical IVs (e.g., *Married*), and click the arrow button to move them to *Factors*.

  - For a polytomous variable, click *Options* and click *Ascending* or *Descending* to use the last or first category, respectively, as the reference category for dummy coding. For a dichotomous variable coded as 0 and 1 typically, *Descending* should be used.

- Select quantitative (e.g., *zParentRole*) IVs, and click the arrow button to move them to *Covariates*.
- Select an offset variable (e.g., *lnYearsFostered*), if appropriate, and click the arrow button to move it to *Offset Variable*.

Model

- Select factors and covariates included as main effects in the model and click the arrow button to move them to *Model*.

Note: You can also use this dialog box to create interaction terms. Click *Help* to get a description of how to do this.

Estimation

- You don't need to change default settings.

Statistics

- Click *Likelihood ratio*, listed under *Chi-Square Statistics*.
- Click *Include exponential parameter estimates*, listed under *Print*.
- For Poisson regression, click *Lagrange multiplier test of scale parameter or negative binomial ancillary parameter* to obtain the test of overdispersion. Don't click this for negative binomial regression.

Estimated Marginal EM Means

- You don't need to change default settings.

Save

- Click *Predicted value of mean response* to save predicted mean counts.
- Click *Predicted value of linear predictor* to save the predicted log of the count.
- Click *Cook's distance* to save Cook's distance.
- Click *Leverage value* to save leverage values.
- Click *Deviance residual* to save deviance residuals.
- Click *Standardized deviance residual* to save standardized deviance residuals.
- Click *OK* to get the results.

Note: After you run the analysis save the data set, which now contains new variables that you can use to create index plots and for other purposes.

Note: SPSS does not have an option to compute a rate for each case. However, after using SPSS to compute and save the predicted mean count for each case (*Predicted value of mean response*) you can use SPSS to compute the rate for each case. For example, if the variable name for the predicted mean count is *MeanPredicted*, and the variable name for the exposure variable is *YearsFostered*, you could use the following syntax to compute the rate for each case:

compute rate = MeanPredicted/YearsFostered.

Excel Workbooks

The names of the following three workbooks correspond to the variables used in the associated Poisson and negative binomial (NB) regression analyses. These workbooks show how we created the figures reported in this chapter for the associated analyses, as well as additional related figures not included.

- (Poisson) zParentRole.xls
- (Poisson) Married & zParentRole.xls
- (NB) zParentRole & zParentRole2.xls
- (NB) Married, zParentRole, MarriedXzParentRole.xls
- (NB) Married & zParentRole.xls

This workbook shows how we created Figure 5.8.

- (Poisson) Observed & Estimated.xls

Glossary

Binary logistic regression Regression model in which the DV is dichotomous; the link function is the logit link; and the assumed underlying
distribution is the binomial distribution. Often referred to simply as
logistic regression or sometimes as *logit regression.*

Censored variables Variables whose observed values are known over some
range, but unknown beyond a certain value because they were recorded
or collected only up (or down) to that value.

Centering Subtracting the sample mean (or some other value such as the
median) of a variable (typically an IV) from each case's score on that
variable.

Common cause Variable that is a cause of both the IV and the DV and,
as such, provides a threat to the validity of the inference that the IV
causes the DV (i.e., the observed relationship between the IV and the
DV is *spurious* because the relationship between the IV and DV is
due to the common cause). Also known as a *confounding variable* or
confound.

Continuous variables Quantitative variables that can take on any value
within the limits of the variables.

Cook's D (distance) Measure of the approximate aggregate change in
estimated regression parameters resulting from deletion of a case.

Count variables Variables that indicate the number of times a particular event occurs, usually within some time period (e.g., number of hospital visits per year), population size (e.g., number of registered sex offenders per 100,000 population), or geographical area (e.g., county or state). Counts are whole numbers that can range from 0 through $+\infty$.

Covariate Quantitative IV.

Cumulative probability Probability that a variable is less than or equal to a particular value.

Curvilinear relationship Relationship between two variables wherein change in the DV differs at different levels of the IV.

Dichotomous variables Variables with two categories indicating that an event has or has not occurred, or that some characteristic is or is not present.

Discrete variables Variables with a finite number of indivisible values; they cannot take on all possible values within the limits of the variable. Discrete variables include dichotomous, polytomous, ordinal, and count variables.

Dummy (indicator) coding Strategy for coding polytomous IVs in which each category is coded as a dichotomous variable (usually 0 or 1); the number of dichotomous variables created and entered into the regression analysis is one less than the number of categories in the polytomous IV; and the excluded category is the reference category against which other categories are compared.

Equidispersion In Poisson regression, the assumption that the variance equals the mean. Underdispersion occurs when the variance is smaller than the mean, and overdispersion occurs when the variance is greater than the mean.

Exponential function Inverse of the natural log, typically abbreviated as e^x or $\exp(x)$.

Exposure Opportunity for an event to occur, such as length of time, population size, geographical area, or other domains of interest.

Factor Categorical/Polytomous IV.

Focal variable See *Interaction*

Full model See *nested models*

General linear model (GLM) Special case of the generalized linear model in which the link function is the identity function; the DV is continuous; it is assumed that the errors are normally distributed and independent with a constant variance; and there is a linear relationship between a linear combination of one or more IVs and one DV. The general linear model includes different statistical models including, for example, the *t*-test, ANOVA, and ANCOVA; these single DV models are subsumed under linear regression.

Generalized linear model (GZLM) Class of regression models in which a linear combination of the IVs (the *linear predictor*) is related to a function (the *link function*) of a continuous or discrete DV. The generalized linear model encompasses and is an extension of the general linear model. It provides a unifying framework for an entire class of regression models; and it subsumes linear regression, binary, multinomial, logistic regression, Poisson and negative binomial regression, and numerous other regression models.

Hierarchical entry See *sequential entry*.

Incidence rate ratio (IRR) In regression models for count variables, the ratio of two rates (e.g., ratio of the rate of occurrence of the DV for males and females).

Independence of irrelevant alternatives (IIA) In multinomial logistic regression, the assumption that the odds of one outcome relative to another are not influenced by other alternatives.

Index plot Scatter plot with case numbers on the horizontal axis, and residuals, influence, or leverage values, for example, on the vertical axis.

Influence Cases whose deletion results in substantial changes to the regression coefficients are said to be *influential*. For example, Cook's D (distance) measures approximate aggregate change in estimated regression parameters resulting from deletion of a case.

Interaction Situation in which the effect of one IV (*focal variable*) is conditional on the values of one or more other IVs (*moderator variable*).

The focal variable is the IV whose effect on the DV is thought to vary as a function of the moderator variable.

Inverse Link Function In the generalized linear model, the reverse of the link function.

Leverage Degree to which a case is unusual in terms of values of the IVs in the regression model.

Likelihood Probability of the observed sample data, given the parameter estimates.

Linear predictor In the generalized linear model, linear combination of the IVs.

Link function In the generalized linear model, the mathematical function (e.g., log) that links the expected value of the DV to a linear combination of IVs.

Logit Natural logarithm of the odds.

Model misspecification Fitting an incorrect model to the data.

Moderator variable See *Interaction*.

Multicollinearity Situation where strong linear relationships exist among IVs.

Multinomial logistic regression Regression model in which the DV is polytomous; the link function is the logit link; and the assumed underlying distribution is the multinomial distribution. Also known as *polytomous or nominal logistic or logit regression* or the *discrete choice model*. Binary logistic regression can be seen as a special case of the multinomial logistic model in which the DV has only two categories.

Negative binomial regression Regression model in which the DV is a count; the link function is the log link; and the assumed underlying distribution is the negative binomial distribution.

Nested models Two models are nested if one (the *reduced model*) is a more restricted version of the other (the *full model*).

Odds Ratio of the probability that some event will occur to the probability that it will not occur.

Odds Ratio (OR) Ratio of the odds of the event for one value of the IV divided by the odds for a different value of the IV, usually a value one unit lower. The OR indicates the amount of change in the odds and the direction of the relationship between an IV and DV.

Offset variable Natural log of an exposure variable.

Ordinal logistic regression Regression model in which the DV is ordinal; the link function is the logit link; and the assumed underlying distribution is the multinomial distribution. Also known as *polytomous or nominal logistic or logit regression* or the *discrete choice model*. Binary logistic regression can be seen as a special case of the ordinal logistic model in which the DV has only two categories.

Ordinal variables Variables that have three or more ordered categories. Sometimes called *ordered categorical variables* or *ordered polytomous variables*.

Outliers Data points that are atypical, in that they are markedly different from the other data in the sample (e.g., the value of an IV may be extremely large or small relative to other values of the IV, or the estimated value of the DV for a case may be very different than the actual value).

Parallel lines assumption In ordinal logistic regression, the assumption that the effect of the IVs is the same for all values of the DV. Also known as *proportional odds, parallel lines, parallel slopes,* or *parallel regression assumption*.

Parameters Numerical characteristics of a population symbolized by Greek letters.

Poisson regression Regression model in which the DV is a count; the link function is the log link; and the assumed underlying distribution is the Poisson distribution.

Polytomous variables Variables that have three or more unordered categories; often called *multicategorical* variables.

Rate In regression models for count variables, a count per unit of time (e.g., number of children adopted per year), population (e.g., number of registered sex offenders per 100,000), geographical area (e.g., number of children below the poverty rate per state), or other type of exposure (sometimes called an *incidence rate*).

Reduced model See *nested models.*

Residual Difference between actual and estimated value of the DV for a case.

Sequential entry Method for entering IVs into a regression equation one at a time, or in blocks, in a predetermined order dictated by the purpose and logic of the research questions. Often called *hierarchical* entry of variables.

Spurious relationship Relationship between two variables that is not due to one variable causing the other (e.g., A causes B), but instead is the result of a third variable (referred to as a *common cause, confound,* or a *confounding variable*) causing both (e.g., C causes A and B) (also known as *spurious correlation*).

Standard scores Scores transformed by subtracting the mean and dividing by the standard deviation for each case. Standard scores always have a mean of zero and a standard deviation of 1. A *z*-score indicates, in standard deviation units, how far and in what direction the value of a score deviates from the distribution's mean. Often these are called *z-scores.*

Statistics Numerical characteristic of a sample symbolized by letters from the Latin alphabet.

Tolerance Measure of multicollinearity that equals the amount of variance in an IV not accounted for by the remaining IVs $(1 - R^2)$.

Truncation Exclusion of cases from the population of interest based on characteristics of the DV.

Variance inflation factor (VIF) Measure of multicollinearity which equals 1/tolerance.

Zero-inflation In Poisson and negative binomial regression, situation where the actual number of zeros is greater than the estimated number.

Appendix A: Description of Data Sets

Chapter 1 Data Set

This is a subset of data described in more detail in Chapter 1. (Most of these can be downloaded from this Web site: http://utcmhsrc.csw. utk.edu/caseyproject/default.htm):

Coakley, T. M., & Orme, J. G. (2006). A psychometric evaluation of the Cultural Receptivity in Fostering Scale. *Research on Social Work Practice, 16*, 520–533.

Orme, J. G., Cherry, D. J., & Cox, M. E. (2006). *Foster Fathers' CFAI-A and CHAP-SR Technical Manual.* Knoxville, TN: University of Tennessee, Children's Mental Health Services Research Center (http://utcmhsrc.csw.utk.edu/caseyproject/).

Orme, J. G., Cherry, D. J., & Rhodes, K. W. (2006). The Help with Fostering Inventory. *Children and Youth Services Review, 28,* 1293–1311.

Orme, J. G., Cox, M. E., Rhodes, K. W., Coakley, T., Cuddeback, G. S., & Buehler, C. (2006). *Casey Home Assessment Protocol (CHAP): Technical manual* (2nd ed.). Knoxville, TN: University of Tennessee, Children's Mental Health Services Research Center (http://utcmhsrc.csw.utk.edu/caseyproject/).

Orme, J. G., Cuddeback, G. S., Buehler, C., Cox, M. E., & Le Prohn, N. (2006). *Casey Foster Applicant Inventory (CFAI) Technical manual* (2nd ed.). Knoxville, TN: University of Tennessee, Children's Mental Health Services Research Center (http://utcmhsrc.csw.utk.edu/caseyproject/).

Orme, J. G., Cuddeback, G. S., Buehler, C., Cox, M. E., & Le Prohn, N. S. (2007). Measuring foster parent potential: Casey Foster Applicant Inventory—Applicant Version. *Research on Social Work Practice, 17,* 77–92.

Chapter 2 Data Set

This is a subset of data described in more detail in Chapter 2. (Most of these can be downloaded from http://utcmhsrc.csw.utk.edu/caseyproject/default.htm):

Cox, M. E., Orme, J. G., & Rhodes, K. W. (2002). Willingness to foster special needs children and foster family utilization. *Children and Youth Services Review, 24*(5), 293–318.

Cox, M. E., Orme, J. G., & Rhodes, K. W. (2003). Willingness to foster children with emotional or behavioral problems. *Journal of Social Service Research, 29*(4), 23–51.

Orme, J. G., Buehler, C., McSurdy, M., Rhodes, K. W., & Cox, M. W. (2003). The foster parent potential scale. *Research on Social Work Practice, 13*(2), 181–207.

Orme, J. G., Buehler, C., McSurdy, M., Rhodes, K. W., Cox, M. E., & Patterson, D. A. (2004). Parental and familial characteristics of family foster care applicants. *Children and Youth Services Review, 26*, 307–329.

Orme, J. G., Buehler, C., Rhodes, K. W., Cox, M. E., McSurdy, M., & Cuddeback, G. (2006). Parental and familial characteristics used in the selection of foster families. *Children and Youth Services Review, 28*, 396–421.

Rhodes, K. W., Orme, J. G., Cox, M. E., & Buehler, C. (2003a). Foster family resources, psychosocial functioning, and retention. *Social Work Research, 27*(3), 135–150.

Rhodes, K. W., Orme, J. G., & McSurdy, M. (2003b). Foster parents' role performance responsibilities: Perceptions of foster mothers, fathers, and workers. *Children and Youth Services Review, 25*(3), 935–964.

Chapter 3 Data Set

This is a subset of data described in more detail in Chapter 3:

Combs-Orme, T., Cain, D., & Wilson, E. (2004). Do maternal concerns at delivery predict parenting stress during infancy? *Child Abuse & Neglect, 28*(4), 377–392.

Wilson, E. E. (2006). *Measuring effort to interview and track mothers of newborns.* Knoxville, TN: University of Tennessee, College of Social Work.

Chapter 4 Data Set

This is a subset of data from the same data set employed in Chapter 1.

Chapter 5 Data Set

This is a subset of data from the same data set employed in Chapter 1.

Appendix B: Logarithms

C onsider the expression 10^2; it is equivalent to 10×10, it equals 100, and it can be read as "10 squared" or "10 to the 2nd power." In this expression, 10 is called the *base* and 2 the *exponent*. Raising a number (the base) to a power (the exponent) is called *exponentiation*.

Logarithms ("logs") are exponents. We will start with base 10 logs because they illustrate the basic logic of logs, and they are relatively easy to understand. Then, we will turn to natural logs because they are important to understanding and interpreting generalized linear models (GZLMs) (see Cohen et al., 2003, and Pampel, 2000, for more detailed, but very readable, discussions of logarithms).

Base 10 Logarithms

Look at Table 8.1. As you can see, 10 must be raised to the power of 1 to get 10, the power of 2 to get 100, the power of 3 to get 1,000, and so forth.

The log of a number (x) to the base 10 equals the power to which 10 must be raised in order to get x. The log of a number to the base 10 is written as $log_{10}(x) = y$, and read as "the log of x to the base 10 equals y." The $\log_{10}$ of 100, for example, is written as: $\log_{10}(100) = 2$, and read as "the log of 100 to the base 10 equals 2."

Table 8.1 Log_{10} Examples

Base (b)	$log_{10}(x)$	x
10	1	10 (10^1)
10	2	100 (10^2)
10	3	1,000 (10^3)
10	4	10,000 (10^4)

In short, when you take the log of a number you know the base and the number you are trying to take the log of (x), and you are trying to find the correct exponent.

Suppose for the moment that the values of 10, 100, 1,000, and 10,000 from Table 8.1 represent income in dollars. The corresponding logs of these numbers (1, 2, 3, and 4) have no intuitive or substantive meaning, so how do you get the original income numbers if you have the logs?

Look again at Table 8.1. As you can see, $10^1 = 10$, $10^2 = 100$, $10^3 = 1,000$, and so on. What we are doing here is raising the base of the log (10) to the value of the log (1, 2, 3, or 4) in order to get the original value of the number (10, 100, 1,000, or 10,000). That is, we "exponentiate" the log. This is known as the *inverse of the log*; sometimes it is called the *antilog*, and it is just the reverse of the log.

In short, when you take the inverse of a log you know the base and the exponent, and you are trying to find the original number (x).

Natural Logarithms

The natural logarithm is used as the link function for the GZLMs discussed in this book. The natural logarithm is a little more difficult to think about, compared to base 10 logarithms. The reason it is a bit more difficult is that the base of the natural logarithm is e, where e is approximately 2.718 (e, after the mathematician Leonhard Euler). However, the basic ideas are the same.

Look at Table 8.2. As you can see, 2.718 must be raised to the power of 1 to get 2.718, the power of 2 to get 7.389, the power of 3 to get 20.086, and so on.

The log of a number (x) to the base of the natural logarithm equals the power to which e must be raised in order to get x. The log of a number

Table 8.2 Natural Logarithm (ln) Examples

Base (b)	ln(x)	x
2.718	1	2.718 (2.718^1)
2.718	2	7.388 (2.718^2)
2.718	3	20.079 (2.718^3)
2.718	4	54.586 (2.718^4)

Note: 2.718 is the approximate base of the natural logarithm.

to the base of the natural logarithm is written as $ln(x) = y$, and read as "the log of x to the base of the natural logarithm equals y." The natural logarithm of 7.389, for example, is written as: $ln(7.389) = 2$, and read as "the natural logarithm of 7.389 equals 2."

As with logarithms to the base 10, when you take the natural logarithm of a number you know the base and the number you are trying to take the log of (x), and you are trying to find the correct exponent.

Look again at Table 8.2. As you can see, $2.718^1 = 2.718$, $2.718^2 = 7.389$, $2.718^3 = 20.086$, and so on. What we are doing here is raising the base of the natural logarithm (2.718) to the value of the log (1, 2, 3, or 4) in order to get the original value of the number (2.718, 7.389, 20.086, 54.598). That is, we "exponentiate" the log. This is the inverse of the natural log (called the **exponential function**), and it can be written as e^x **or exp(x)**. For example, the base of the natural log raised to a power of 2 equals 7.39, and this expression can be written as $e^2 = 7.39$ or $exp(2) = 7.39$, and read as "the base of the natural log raised to the power of 2 equals 7.39."

As with logarithms to the base 10, when you take the inverse of a natural logarithm you know the base and the exponent, and you are trying to find the original number (x).

References

Agresti, A. (2007). *An introduction to categorical data analysis* (2nd ed.). New York: John Wiley & Sons.

Bagley, S. C., White, H., & Golomb, B. A. (2001). Logistic regression in the medical literature: Standards for use and reporting, with particular attention to one medical domain. *Journal of Clinical Epidemiology, 54,* 979–985.

Barth, R. P., Lloyd, E. C., Green, R. L., James, S., Leslie, L. K., & Landsverk, J. (2007). Predictors of placement moves among children with and without emotional and behavioral disorders. *Journal of Emotional and Behavioral Disorders, 15*(1), 46–55.

Borooah, V. K. (2001). *Logit and probit: Ordered and multinomial models.* Thousand Oaks, CA: Sage.

Borooah, V. K. (2002). *Logit and probit: Ordered and multinomial models.* Thousand Oaks, CA: Sage.

Cheng, S., & Long. J. S. (2007). Testing for IIA in the multinomial logit model. *Sociological Methods & Research, 35,* 583–600.

Choi, N. G. (2003). Nonmarried aging parents and their adult children's characteristics associated with transitions into and out of intergenerational coresidence. *Journal of Gerontological Social Work, 40*(3), 7–29.

Cohen, J., Cohen, P., West, S. G., & Aiken, L. S. (2003). *Applied multiple regression/correlation analysis for the behavioral sciences* (3rd ed.). Mahwah, NJ: Lawrence Erlbaum.

Cole, S.A., & Eamon, M. K. (2007). Predictors of depressive symptoms among foster caregivers. *Child Abuse and Neglect, 31,* 295–310.

Combs-Orme, T., & Cain, D. S. (2008). Predictors of mothers' use of spanking with their infants. *Child Abuse and Neglect, 32*, 649–657.

Combs-Orme, T., Cain, D., & Wilson, E. (2004). Do maternal concerns at delivery predict parenting stress during infancy? *Child Abuse & Neglect, 28*(4), 377–392.

Courtney, M. (1998). Correlates of social worker decisions to seek treatment-oriented out-of-home care. *Children and Youth Services Review, 20*(4), 281–304.

Cox, M. E., Orme, J. G., & Rhodes, K. W. (2003). Willingness to foster children with emotional or behavioral problems. *Journal of Social Service Research, 29*, 23–51.

Dattalo, P. (2008). *Determining sample size. Balancing power, precision, and practicality.* Oxford: Oxford University Press.

DeMaris, A. (2004). *Regression with social data: Modeling continuous and limited response variables.* Hoboken, NJ: John Wiley & Sons.

Diwan, S., Jonnalagadda, S. S., & Balaswamy, S. (2004). Resources predicting positive and negative affect during the experience of stress: A study of older Asian Indian immigrants in the United States. *The Gerontologist, 44*(5), 605–614.

Dunteman, G. H., & Ho, M. R. (2006). *An introduction to generalized linear models.* Thousand Oaks, CA: Sage.

Fox, J. (2008). *Applied regression analysis and generalized linear models* (2nd ed.). Thousand Oaks, CA: Sage.

Gelman, A., & Hill, J. (2007). *Data analysis using regression and multi-level/hierarchical models.* New York: Cambridge University Press.

Gill, J. (2001). *Generalized linear models: A unified approach.* Thousand Oaks, CA: Sage.

Greene, W. H. (2008). *Econometric analysis* (6th ed.). Upper Saddle River, NJ: Prentice Hall.

Hardin, J., & Hilbe, J. (2007). *Generalized linear models and extensions* (2nd ed.). College Station, TX: Stata Press.

Hilbe, J. M. (2007). *Negative binomial regression.* Cambridge: Cambridge University Press.

Hoffmann, J. P. (2004). *Generalized linear models: An applied approach.* Boston: Pearson.

Hosmer, D. W., & Lemeshow, S. (2000). *Applied logistic regression* (2nd ed.). New York: John Wiley.

Jaccard, J. (2001). *Interaction effects in logistic regression.* Thousand Oaks, CA: Sage.

Keith, T. Z. (2006). *Multiple regression and beyond.* Boston, MA: Allyn & Bacon.

Kleinbaum, D. G., & Klein, M. (2002). *Logistic regression: A self-learning text* (2nd ed.). New York, NY: Springer.

Leslie, L. K., Landsverk, J., Ezzet-Loftstrom, R., Tschann, J. M., Slymen, D. J., & Garland, A. F. (2000). Children in foster care: Factors influencing outpatient mental health service use. *Child Abuse and Neglect, 24*(4), 465–476.

Le Prohn, N. S. (1994). The role of the kinship foster parent: A comparison of the role conceptions of relative and non-relative foster parents. *Children and Youth Services Review, 16*(1/2), 65–84.

Litwin, H., & Zoabi, S. (2004). A multivariate examination of explanations for the occurrence of elder abuse. *Social Work Research, 28*(3), 133–142.

Long, J. S. (1997). *Regression models for categorical and limited dependent variables.* Thousand Oaks, CA: Sage.

Long, J. S., & Cheng, S. (2004). Regression models for categorical outcomes. In M. Hardy & A. Bryman (Eds.), *Handbook of data analysis* (pp. 259–284). Thousand Oaks, CA: Sage.

Long, J. S., & Freese, J. (2006). *Regression models for categorical dependent variables using Stata* (2nd ed.). College Station, TX: Stata Press.

McCullagh, P., & Nelder, J.A. (1989). *Generalized linear models* (2nd ed.). London: Chapman & Hall.

McCulloch, C. E., Searle, S. R., & Neuhaus, J. M. (2008). *Generalized, linear, and mixed models.* New York: John Wiley & Sons.

Menard, S. (2001). *Applied logistic regression analysis* (2nd ed.). Thousand Oaks, CA: Sage.

Norusis, M. J. (2006). *SPSS 15.0 statistical procedures companion.* Upper Saddle River, NJ: Prentice Hall.

Norusis, M. J. (2007). *SPSS 15.0 advanced statistical procedures companion.* Upper Saddle River, NJ: Prentice Hall.

Nunnally, J. C., & Bernstein, I. H. (1994). *Psychometric theory* (3rd ed.). New York: McGraw-Hill.

O'Connell, A. (2006). *Logistic regression models for ordinal response variables.* Thousand Oaks, CA: Sage.

Orme, J. G., & Buehler, C. (2001). Introduction to multiple regression for categorical and limited dependent variables. *Social Work Research, 25,* 49–61.

Orme, J. G., Buehler, C., Rhodes, K. W., Cox, M. E., McSurdy, M., & Cuddeback, G. (2006). Parental and familial characteristics used in the selection of foster families. *Children and Youth Services Review, 28,* 396–421.

Orme, J. G., Cuddeback, G. S., Buehler, C., Cox, M. E., & Le Prohn, N. S. (2007). Measuring foster parent potential: Casey Foster Applicant Inventory—Applicant Version. *Research on Social Work Practice, 17,* 77–92.

Oxford, M. L., Gilchrist, L. D., Gillmore, M. R., & Lohr, M. J. (2006). Predicting variation in the life course of adolescent mothers as they enter adulthood. *Journal of Adolescent Health, 39,* 20–26.

Pampel, F. (2000). *Logistic regression: A primer*. Thousand Oaks, CA: Sage.

Pedhazur, E. J. (1997). *Multiple regression in behavioral research: Explanation and prediction* (3rd ed.). Fort Worth, TX: Holt, Rinehart & Winston.

Peduzzi, P., Concato, J., Kemper, E., Holford, T. R., & Feinstein, A. R. (1996). A simulation study of the number of events per variable in logistic regression analysis. *Journal of Clinical Epidemiology, 49*, 1373–1379.

Piantadosi, S. (2005). *Clinical trials: A methodologic perspective* (2nd ed.). New York: John Wiley & Sons.

Rhodes, K. W., Orme, J. G., Cox, M. E., & Buehler, C. (2003a). Foster family resources, psychosocial functioning, and retention. *Social Work Research, 27*, 135–150.

Rhodes, K. W., Orme, J. G., & McSurdy, M. (2003b). Foster parents' role performance responsibilities: Perceptions of foster mothers, fathers, and workers. *Children and Youth Services Review, 25*(3), 935–964.

Rishel, C. W., Greeno, C., Marcus, S. C., Shear, M. K., & Anderson, C. (2005). Use of the Child Behavior Checklist as a diagnostic screening tool in community mental health. *Research on Social Work Practice, 15*(2), 195–203.

Rosenthal, J. A. (1996). Qualitative descriptors of strength of association and effect size. *Journal of Social Service Research, 21*, 37–59.

Scott, J. (2006). Job satisfaction among TANF leavers. *Journal of Sociology & Social Welfare, XXXIII*(3), 127–149.

Shadish, W. R., Cook, T. D., & Campbell, D. T. (2002). *Experimental and quasi-experimental designs for generalized causal inference*. Boston: Houghton Mifflin.

Smokowski, P. R., Mann, E. A., Reynolds, A. J., & Fraser, M. W. (2004). Childhood risk and protective factors and late adolescent adjustment in inner city minority youth. *Children and Youth Services Review, 26*, 63–91.

SPSS advanced models 16.0 (2007). SPSS: Chicago, IL.

Stevens, J. P. (2001). *Applied multivariate statistics for the social sciences* (4th ed.). Mahwah, NJ: Lawrence Erlbaum.

Vittinghoff, E., & McCulloch, C. E. (2006). Relaxing the rule of ten events per variable in logistic and Cox regression. *American Journal of Epidemiology, 165*, 710–718.

Wilson, E. E. (2006). *Measuring effort to interview and track mothers of newborns*. Knoxville, TN: University of Tennessee, College of Social Work.

Zuravin, S., Orme, J. G., & Hegar, R. (1994). Predicting severity of child abuse injury with ordinal probit regression. *Social Work Research and Abstracts, 18*, 131–138.

Index